PRAISE FOR NEVER TOO LATE

"It is the kind of book you will return to again and again, and Claire Cook is the kind of writer you will only want more from."
—*Stephanie Burns, BookPerfume.com*

Never Too Late resonated with me on a level that I didn't expect. Still at this moment, I am reviewing all the notes that I took while reading the book."
—*Victoria Colotta, artbookscoffee.com*

"If you need a personal cheerleader to help you along your road to reinvention, then I highly recommend this book."
—*Laurie Nerat, Looking on the Sunnyside*

"It's a thought-provoking, inspiring book. If you've thought about changing your career and following your passion, Cook's book just might provide the needed push."—*Lesa's Book Critiques*

"The book is about change and opportunity—and how to grab them."—*Pamela Kramer, National Book Reviewer, Examiner.com*

BOOKS BY CLAIRE COOK

Shine On: How To Grow Awesome Instead of Old
Never Too Late: Your Roadmap to Reinvention

Must Love Dogs (#1)
Must Love Dogs: New Leash on Life (#2)
Must Love Dogs: Fetch You Later (#3)
Must Love Dogs: Bark & Roll Forever (#4)
and stay tuned for *Must Love Dogs* Book 5!

The Wildwater Walking Club
Best Staged Plans
Seven Year Switch
Summer Blowout
Life's a Beach
Multiple Choice
Time Flies
Wallflower in Bloom
Ready to Fall

NEVER TOO LATE

Your Roadmap to Reinvention
(without getting lost along the way)

Claire Cook

Marshbury Beach Books

Marshbury Beach Books
Book Layout: The Book Designer
Author Photo: Stuart Wilson
Cover Photo: Lev Kropotov
Never Too Late/ Claire Cook
ISBN 978-0-9899210-8-4

For reinventors everywhere

"It is never too late to be what you might have been."

–George Eliot

JUMPING IN

Reinvention is the theme of my novels. It's the story of my life. Or at least my midlife. Wherever I go and whatever I do—workshops, women's conferences, book events, interviews, visits with friends—it's pretty much what we end up talking about.

I certainly never set out to try to become the mother of reinvention, as a former editor used to call me in a twist on that old band from the '60s, The Mothers of Invention. In fact, it feels more like we're all in this together, muddling along as we try to figure out how to get to that life we really thought we'd be living by now. Perhaps the best thing I have to offer is that I made every mistake in the book and came so incredibly close to never dusting off that buried dream of mine. And now here I am, living the life I almost missed.

Over the course of eleven novels and fourteen years, I've cheered on lots of other women (and a few good men), sharing everything I can think of that might help them in their own reinventions. And I've been lucky enough to hear some incredible reinvention stories, too. Passed them along. Watched them inspire others just when they needed it.

On this particular trip, as I land at the Cancún airport, wade through Mexican customs, climb into a waiting shuttle van, and ride a ferry northeast through turquoise Caribbean ocean to beautiful Isla Mujeres (Island of Women) to give the keynote (on reinvention!) at an annual International Women's Day weekend conference called We Move Forward, it hits me.

Even if I travel and travel and travel, I might never meet you in person. I think it's time to share my journey with you anyway, in hopes that it might help you with your own.

I bump my seriously over-packed suitcase down the ramp and step onto the island of women, ready to soak up the sunshine and stories.

QUICK SUGGESTION

We're all different—our goals and styles and personalities. So if something I say in the pages that follow doesn't resonate for you, ignore it. Turn the page, paper or virtual. Move on.

But if it provokes a strong negative reaction—*that Claire Cook has no idea what she's talking about* or *that's the most ridiculous thing I've ever heard*—or if it just really pisses you off, write it down before you move on. Bookmark it. Highlight it. Mark it with a Post-It.

In a week or two, go back and take another look. I don't know about you, but sometimes what I really, really need to hear to get where I'm going is the hardest thing to hear, the thing that initially infuriates me the most.

ROADMAP TO THE STARS

If there were a roadmap to success, we'd all be following it. We'd have it saved on our GPS or made into a poster hanging over our bed. Every book would be a bestseller, every movie would be a mega hit, every blog would have a gazillion followers, every restaurant would have a line snaking out to the street.

There are people who will give you bullet points, action plans, absolute secrets to success. But the truth as I see it is that nobody really knows. What works for you might not work for me. What works tomorrow might not work the next year, or even the next day. If it were easy to be successful, we'd all be doing it.

So you have to create your own roadmap. You have to designate your starting point, figure out your destination, work around the inevitable detours and potholes and traffic jams. You have to stay on the road, even if you don't feel like it. Even if you really need to pee.

It's a huge leap of faith. It's a ton of work.

But it feels awesome when you get there.

REINVENTION DEFINITION

The Merriam-Webster Dictionary presents a range of possibilities when it defines *reinvent*: "to make major changes or improvements to (something) . . . to present (something) in a different or new way . . . to remake or redo completely . . . to bring into use again."

So make yours a massive, earth-shattering change. Or just the perfect tweak to your existing life. It's your reinvention and you can do it any way you want to.

BURIED DREAM

I've known I was a writer since I was three. I was one of eight kids, and when you grow up in those great big families, you desperately want something that's just yours to make you feel special, to separate you from the pack. I grabbed writer.

My mother entered me in a contest to name the Fizzies whale, and I won in my age group. It's quite possible that mine was the only entry in the three-and-under category, since Cutie Fizz was enough to win my family a six-month supply of Fizzies tablets (root beer was the best flavor) and half a dozen white plastic whale-embellished mugs with turquoise removable handles. (Completely off-topic, but I would give anything to find those mugs again. If you ever see them on eBay or at a yard/garage/tag sale, please let me know!)

When I was six, my first story was published in the Little People's Page in the Sunday paper (about Hot Dog, the family dachshund, even though we had a beagle at the time, the first clue that I'd be a novelist and not a journalist) and at sixteen I had my first front-page feature in the local weekly. I also wrote really bad poetry in high school that I thought was so profound—

yep, I was *that* girl. I majored in film and creative writing in college, studying with some big name writers who gave me lots of positive feedback.

I'd been on this writing road for most of my short life, and it seemed like a straight shot to my destination. I fully expected that the day after graduation, I would go into labor and a brilliant novel would emerge, fully formed, like giving birth.

It didn't happen. Instead, I choked. I panicked. I guess I'd learned how to write, but I didn't know *what* to write. I felt like an imposter. So, despite all expectations, especially mine, I didn't write much of anything over the next couple decades. Even the prospect of writing a thank-you note would throw me into full-blown anxiety mode. (If I still owe you one from way back then, sorry.)

Hindsight 20/20, I can see that I just hadn't found my stories yet. I write about real women—their quirky lives, their crazy families and friendships and relationships, what they want and what's keeping them from getting it. I simply needed to live more of my own life before I could accumulate enough experience to write my novels. If I could give my younger self some really good advice, it would be not to beat myself up for the next twenty years.

But I did. Most of the time I felt a low-grade kind of angst about not living up to my potential. I did my best to ignore it, but sometimes it would bubble up and I'd feel gut-wrenchingly awful. I tried my hardest to bury the feelings, to forget about my dream.

But it never went away. Writing a novel remained the thing I wanted to do more than anything else in the whole wide world, as well as the thing I was most afraid of.

So I did some other creative things. I wrote shoe ads for an in house advertising department for five weeks right out of college, became continuity director of a local radio station for a year or two, taught aerobics and did some choreography, worked as a bartender, helped a friend with landscape design, wrote a few freelance magazine pieces, took some more detours.

Eventually, I had two children and followed them to their artsy little school as a teacher. I meant to stay for a year or two, but somehow I stayed for sixteen. Sixteen years. I taught everything from multicultural games and dance to open ocean rowing to creative writing. I loved the kids and even won the Massachusetts Governor's Fitness Award for innovative programming. But all along I was hiding from my true passion, the thing I was born to do.

And then one day, propelled by the fierce, unrelenting energy of midlife, the dream burst to the surface again. I was in my forties, sitting with a group of swim moms (and a few good dads) at 5:30 A.M. My daughter was swimming back and forth and back and forth on the other side of a huge glass window during the first of two daily practices that bracketed her school day and my workday as a teacher.

The parental conversation in the wee hours of that morning, as we sat bleary-eyed, cradling our Styrofoam cups of coffee and watching our kids, was all about training and form and speed, who was coming on at the perfect time, who was in danger of peaking before championships, even who just might have a shot at Olympic trial times.

In my mind, I stepped back and listened. *Whoa,* I thought, *we really need to get a life.*

And right at that moment it hit me with the force of a poolside tidal wave that I was the one who needed to get a life. A new one, the one I'd meant to have all along. I was not getting any younger, and I was in serious danger of living out my days without ever once going for it. Without even *trying* to achieve my lifelong dream of writing a novel. Suddenly, *not* writing a book became more painful than pushing past all that fear and procrastination and actually writing it.

So, for the next six months, through one long cold New England winter and into the spring, I wrote a draft of my first novel, sitting in my minivan outside my daughter's swim practice. It sold to the first publisher who asked to read it. Lots of terrific books by talented authors take a long time to sell, so maybe I got lucky. I've also considered that perhaps if you procrastinate as long as I did, you get to skip some of the awful stages on the path to wherever it is you're going and just cut to the chase.

But another way to look at it is that there were only three things standing in my way all those years: me, myself and I.

My first novel, *Ready to Fall,* was published when I was forty-five. At fifty, I walked the red carpet at the Hollywood premiere of the movie adaptation of my second novel, *Must Love Dogs*, starring Diane Lane and John Cusack. I'm now an actual bestselling author of a whole bunch of novels. Not many days go by that I don't take a deep breath and remind myself that this is the career I almost didn't have.

REINVENTION INTERSECTION

I think we all have that sweet spot—the place where the life we want to live and our ability intersect. For some, the trick is finding it. If you're one of those people, you're still trying to figure out what you want to be when you grow up—at thirty, at fifty, at seventy.

For others, like me, deep down inside you already know what you want, so it's about finding the courage to dig up that dream and dust it off. It's not too late. Dreams don't have an expiration date. Not even a best by date. If it's still your dream, it's still your dream.

When I first began speaking about reinvention, I used to joke that, at my age, it's a good thing my buried dream was to become a novelist and not a rock star. I'd get a nice laugh and go on to say that you can write your first book at any age, and that so many other novelists, especially women, have been late-bloomers like me.

And then one summer morning I find myself on Cape Cod at a launch breakfast for my latest novel. It's a gorgeous beachy day. The event is being hosted by one of my favorite independent bookstores, and the restaurant is packed with smiling women. When I finish speaking, I move to a table piled with impressive stacks of my beautiful new book.

It's a long, lovely signing line, and I take a moment to chat with each person and to write something special in her book. At the very end is a woman about my age, give or take. I smile, sign her book, thank her for coming.

She looks me right in the eyes. "About that thing you said? Well, I'm still hoping to make it as a musician."

If I don't gasp, I feel like it. Ack—thinking about it still makes me blush. There I am talking about having the courage to go for it, and in doing so, I'm stomping all over another woman's dream. So what if there aren't many midlife women breaking into the music business. Who am I to say she won't be the one to beat the odds? Who am I to rain on her parade?

I apologize up and down and all over the place, and I've never made that reference again, unless I'm describing my own gaffe as I am here. Years later I still think of that woman. I keep waiting for her to show up as a contestant on *The Voice*, or to see her and her kick-butt midlife band on a video that's gone viral on YouTube. I hope the roadmap she's following lands her smack dab in the middle of her dream.

If you're not sure which category you fall into—lifelong buried dream or what do I want to be when I grow up—take some time to think about it. A few minutes. A few months. Whatever you need.

What was that thing you wanted to do before life—bills, kids, aging parents, grocery shopping, laundry—

got in the way? What did you love to do as a child, before the raging hormones of adolescence kicked in and turned you into a lovesick puppy? What's the thing you'd do in a heartbeat if you didn't think it was too late?

What makes you happy? What floats your boat? What would you like a day in your life to feel like? What puts you so in the zone that hours and hours pass and you've barely glanced at the clock? If money were no issue, what is the thing you feel so passionately about that you'd do it for free? What do you care about enough to want to put in the time required to get better and better at it?

Whatever it is, I think you have to do it because you love it, not for fame or fortune, or even a movie and a chance to hang out with John Cusack. In my little corner, I often hear from aspiring writers who are so focused on seeing their book out in the world (where they'll travel for book tour, what they'll wear in their author photo) that they're not putting in the time on the important thing—the writing.

You have to love the words (guitar/clay), and be willing to dive back in again and again, as many times as it takes, until your book (music/pottery) is as good as it can be. I'm grateful that I don't have to anymore, but I would absolutely find a way to write my next novel even if I still had to support myself with another job, or jobs. Each book teaches me so much—about the characters, about the world they live in, about myself.

YOUR NOTEBOOK

John Lennon once said that whenever he had an idea, he'd scribble it on a piece of paper and throw it in a drawer. When the drawer was full, he knew it was time for a new album.

I love that. It speaks to me of the magic of creation, the way if you trust in the process, forget about all the bells and whistles and just put in the work, disparate things can eventually come together and become something far greater than the sum of their parts.

I prefer notebooks to scraps of loose paper. I keep them wherever the ideas come—in the car, on my bedside table, under my cell phone, next to the elliptical machine, near the shower. I used to think it was a Murphy's Law kind of thing—that my best ideas showed up only when writing them down might mean a soggy notebook or a near fender-bender.

But now I believe ideas come in these places simply because you've stopped trying too hard. You've walked away from the computer, stopped attempting to micromanage your brain, and *abracadabra*, that brilliant idea just pops up out of nowhere.

You think you'll remember it. It's so genius, how could you possibly forget? And before you know it, it's gone forever.

Sure, you could use your smartphone or your iPad to write it down. But there's something so basic and unthreatening about a notebook. And words on paper are physical, too, like the first brick and mortar building blocks to your dream.

Whenever I get stuck while I'm writing a novel, I gather up my notebooks, curl up on my bed or stretch out on the floor of my office, and flip through them. Invariably, I find just the thing, as if some part of me *knew* I'd need this idea—or snippet of dialog, or random observation—a little further down the road to spur me on.

Personally, I don't do so well with fancy notebooks. When I was in college, someone gave me a green leather notebook with my name engraved on the cover in gold. I still have it, but I've never written word one in it.

On the set of the *Must Love Dogs* movie, I sat in my director's chair and jotted down every detail I observed, not sure how I'd use any of it, but so awed by being a fly on the Hollywood wall that I didn't want to forget a thing.

I filled the only notebook I'd brought with me, moved on to hotel stationery, transitioned to the back of the daily call sheets. The producers kept laughing and saying, "Somebody get Claire some more paper." One day they gave me a beautiful deep blue leather notebook. It was a lovely gesture, but I only pretended to write in it. It was too perfect, too fancy, like the good china people save for special occasions.

I like the composition notebooks you can buy at your local dollar store. They remind me of elementary school, which is oddly soothing and makes me feel nostalgic. And also a little bit badass that I'm all grown up now and don't have to stay between the lines anymore. I don't have to practice my penmanship, study for spelling tests, diagram sentences. I'm glad I have those rock-solid, old-fashioned, nun-powered skills as part of my tool kit, but I can write whatever I want now. So there.

I also love smaller notebooks that are just the right size to tuck into a purse or a pocket, tiny notebooks that clip onto your keychain, flip-flop shaped notebooks, notebooks covered in chevron patterns or polka dots or animal prints. They don't take themselves too seriously. They're fun. They're not intimidating.

At almost every event since my first book came out, I've raffled off a notebook to bring an extra dose of good luck to one person in the room. Every so often an email will pop into my website inbox from someone who won the notebook in Florida or Colorado or Connecticut. *I won the notebook! And guess what? I finished my book!* Or opened that salvage warehouse. Or started that cable show. Or blog. Or shop on Etsy.

It always gives me goose bumps.

So get a notebook, college-lined and utilitarian. Just the first one that calls out to you.

Because it's not the notebook—it's what you do with it. And I suggest that whenever you have a brilliant idea or discover a great resource or stumble across anything that might help you on your particular road to reinvention, you simply write it down. Don't structure it like a diary or a gratitude journal, or try to pound it into submission by forcing yourself to write in it every day, or three times a week, or when the moon is full.

Let your notebook take on a life of its own. And one day when you're stuck at a crossroads or you hit a detour, flipping through it might be just the thing you need to get back on track.

MEANWHILE, BACK ON THE ISLA

In case you have an image of me diva hopping off to Mexico, my designer scarf blowing in the wind, here's how it really goes: I wake up at 5 A.M. to jump in the shower and do my final pack before I make my way to the Atlanta airport. Lots of book tours have taught me the hard way to travel with just a carry-on. So many events in so little time mean that if you check a bag and it gets lost, you could be speaking without makeup and wearing your stretched-out yoga pants to an auditorium full of people before it catches up to you.

I've learned to roll each piece of clothing into a tight little cylinder and stand it up on one end in the suitcase. Try it—you can jam in an amazing amount of clothing this way, and when you finish, your carry-on will look like a freshly opened pack of clothing cigarettes.

But I'll be on Isla Mujeres for five days, and Mexico seems to be one of the few destinations in the world where the airline lets you check one suitcase free. How can I resist? I roll enough summery clothing to open a small boutique, and cram it all into my biggest suitcase. I stuff almost every piece of underwear and pair of flip-flops I own around the clothing. I add full-size containers of moisturizer and sunscreen, plus makeup that will only end up melting off my face in the island heat and humidity. I top it off with the funky sun hat my son has just given me for my birthday, not that I've ever once in my life worn a sun hat.

Then I start getting a little bit crazy. A mini flat iron for my hair that my daughter made me buy and which I've yet to use. A Ziploc Baggie of my favorite Trader Joe's coffee and a few unbleached filters, just in case the coffee in my hotel room is lacking. A little juice box-like container of milk so I don't have to contaminate good coffee with bad coffee creamer. A couple of tiny bottles of wine, because there might not be any alcohol in Mexico. Breakfast bars. Teensy packages of nuts. As much bottled water as I can wiggle in between my army of tightly rolled clothing soldiers.

I know that the We Move Forward conference will be giving each participant a blank journal with her registration packet. I don't want to take away from that, so I decide not to bring one of my lucky giveaway notebooks. Instead I'll raffle off as many of my books as I can fit. I also bring a big, heavy stack of bookmarks with pictures of my book covers, as well as my website and social networking contact info on them.

I know I'm in trouble when I can barely roll my suitcase to my front door, let alone lift it. A quick Internet check tells me that the fee for an overweight suitcase is ridiculous, and the whole thing is beginning to feel like a bait and switch: Suck in the silly tourist with the promise of a free suitcase, and then once she's got her heart set on bringing everything she owns, snatch it away.

But wait. Maybe fifty pounds just feels heavier in my panicked condition. A weight/reality check seems to be in order. I'm certainly not dragging the suitcase all the way to the bathroom, so I bring the bathroom scale to the suitcase. My husband, who is planning to drive me to the airport, I hope in time to actually make the flight, helps me hoist the suitcase onto the scale.

Alas, the scale wants to register the suitcase as another family member before it will cough up the weight. It also wants to know the suitcase's fitness regimen, its diet goals, its astrological sign. I text my son to find out how to override this foolishness. He tells me it will be faster to just go with it. Eventually I find out that my suitcase is morbidly obese, weighing in at a whopping sixty-three pounds. It is also a Sagittarius and needs to eat fewer carbs and consider taking a Zumba class.

I pitch the bottled water, random cylinders of clothing, half the flip-flops, all but six of my books. Another weigh-in and I let go of a couple of my own personal notebooks, the flat iron, all but one of the teensy bottles of wine.

Not until I jump into the car does it hit me that in the time it took me to over-pack and then purge, I could have written a good-size chunk of my next novel.

Here it is again, the lesson that my life seems to want to teach me over and over again: Sometimes the biggest thing you can do to find your next chapter is to get out of your own way.

COMMITMENT TIME

If you're still suffering from notebook-commitment issues, now's the time to power through. Choose your notebook. Do eeny-meeny-miny-moe if you have to.

Okay, done. Moving on. Blank notebooks can be surprisingly intimidating. So maybe scribble on the first couple pages of yours so it's not a virgin anymore. Or write a few lines of Every Good Woman Deserves Reinvention. Or fudge. Or just doodle. Or even make some bullet points if you simply can't help yourself.

Now turn the page. If you're like me, you already know what you want. A book. Or a speaking gig. A blog. A consulting career. A web startup. Your own show on the Amazon network. To learn to play the guitar. So write it down—the thing you want, the dream you've buried. It's not time to announce it to the world yet. In fact, there are some pretty good reasons why you might not want to, which I'll get into later. But now's the time to admit it to the most important person. Yourself.

If you're one of the people still not sure what they want to be when they grow up, that's okay. Maybe even a good thing. As Stephen Colbert said, "If we'd all stuck with our first dream, the world would be overrun with cowboys and princesses."

But I hope by now you're spending some quality time thinking about it. You're cruising the Internet looking for ideas, doing random Google searches, reading everything you can get your hands on. And at the same time, I hope, as the poet Ann Sexton said, you "put your ear down close to your soul and listen hard."

When something calls out to you, try it on for size. Take a class. Experiment. You don't have to be good at it yet—that takes time and hard work. But you have to love it enough to *want* to be good at it.

Okay, time's up. Contemplation is a wonderful thing, but too much and suddenly you've got a bad case of analysis paralysis. So pick something. It doesn't have to be the right thing, the perfect thing, your ultimate reinvention. It might turn out to be a detour. And that's all right. You're allowed to make a mistake. You're allowed to embarrass yourself. You're allowed to hit a dead end. The important thing is that you commit to it and follow it through as far as it can go.

Because if you don't have a destination, you can't get there. One of my favorite Lily Tomlin lines describes this syndrome perfectly: "I always wanted to be some-body, but I should have been more specific." Write that in your notebook if you need to.

The other important thing is that you pick just one thing and don't let yourself get derailed. Creative people are good at lots of things. But if you choose one and focus all your energy and creativity on it, you'll go from good to better. And that singular focus can make all the difference when it comes to reinventing your life.

I can't tell you how many times over the years someone has come up to me after one of my events to tell me about her partially completed drafts of two novels and three short stories, not to mention her almost-finished screenplay, all of which she's abandoned because she just got a great idea for a children's book. Which she's going to dive right into as soon as she finishes taking a ceramics class.

I think there are a couple of factors at work here. First, the structure and energy that goes into choreographing a dance routine is not all that different from weaving a tapestry or designing a garden or writing a comedy skit or creating a mosaic. This interconnectedness makes for a great meditation or a fascinating discussion, but it can also lead to a bad case of shiny object syndrome.

Been there. I've watched one mesmerizing possibility after another whirl by while I thought, *I want to try that, I can do that, ooh, what about this, or that, andthatandthatandthatandthatandthat.* And still, halfway through every single novel I write, I struggle not to jump to a "better" idea, because the grass is always so much greener around the book I'm not really writing.

As Steven Covey said, "You have to decide what your highest priorities are and have the courage—pleasantly, smilingly, nonapologetically, to say 'no' to other things. And the way you do that is by having a bigger 'yes' burning inside."

For me at least, some of the urge to jump around comes from fear. Once you commit to something and finish it, you have to put it out there and see what the world has to say about it. That part never gets any easier. But you do it anyway, because that's how you learn and grow, and how you get better at that place where your urge to reinvent your life and your ability intersect.

And even on your worst days, you'll be lucky enough to be living your dream.

JUST SAY YES

Janeen Halliwell is the founder of We Move Forward. The women's conference is in its third year, which means that Janeen is three years into her own reinvention. Scheduled to coincide with International Women's Day in early March, We Move Forward is a three-day experience designed to help women "take their ordinary to extraordinary, buoyed by the strength and encouragement of other women, who just like them, are moving forward." It began as a way for Janeen and her mother, Mary MacSporran, to move forward in their own lives after losing Janeen's father and Mary's husband, Scotty, to pancreatic cancer.

We Move Forward is a true passion for Janeen. She's investing boatloads of energy, as well as her own money, into making this dream come true. She books the biggest venue on tiny Isla Mujeres, with spectacular ocean views. She brings in a varied and interesting assortment of speakers, and she keeps the price down so that ordinary women can actually afford to go. She includes mindful movement classes and even mini massages. Breakfasts, happy hours, dinners. For every ten paying participants, a local Mexican woman gets to attend for free. The conference is structured so that you could go alone and feel comfortable, or arrange to meet up with friends there and reconnect.

I'm thrilled that Janeen has invited me to give the keynote. But still, as soon as I say yes, I wish I'd said no. It isn't about We Move Forward. This is the same buyer's remorse I get when I say yes to anything that will take me away from my computer, my deadlines, my safe little world. And then once I get to wherever it is I wish I'd said no to, I'm always glad I made myself go.

Over the years I've learned to say yes when I know I should, to lock myself in so I can't wiggle out, to ignore my self-limiting second-guessing.

I'm reminded how common these feelings are when I tell two friends on opposite sides of the country that I think the conference would be right up their alleys. *You should go*, I say, in two separate conversations. In almost exactly the same words, these two very different women tell me that it sounds great and they'll give it some serious thought. I wait and eventually they both wiggle out the way I'd like to. Too much going on right now. Maybe next year.

What I know about both these women is that they're caretakers, always the first to step up when somebody needs them, always there in a crisis. They'd hop on a plane in a second for their kids, for their aging parents. Even for me, I'm pretty sure. I joke to one of them that I should have told her I *needed* her to come with me. She laughs and tells me I've totally got her number.

I get it. I fight it all the time. But if you truly want to reinvent your life, you're going to have to learn to say yes. Even if it feels selfish. Or scary.

In the end, I'm glad I go alone, at least this time. I think I'll make more friends, experience it more fully. It will push me further out of my own comfort zone, which is where the growth always happens.

When my ferry docks at Isla Mujeres, Janeen is already hosting the pre-conference happy hour meet and greet under a restaurant *palapa*, an open air structure with a roof made of dried palm leaves. So she sends two women, her mother Mary and Janna Zinzi, to meet me.

I'm still a bit rocky from the turbulence the plane hit as we descended from the sky to the Yucatan Peninsula. It seemed to last forever and it was rough enough that several people on the plane screamed. Fear of flying isn't on my own fairly extensive anxiety list, but fear of vomiting is. I've only had the experience in the air once, on book tour, when a bolt of lightning just missed the wing of the tiny plane I was on, and a thunderstorm forced us to make an emergency landing in a field in northern Michigan. I know for a fact that they don't make those barf bags big enough, so I'm grateful to have avoided a repeat performance.

But my stomach remains in a tight knot, and I've been doing the long slow breathing thing ever since, trying to get it to settle down—throughout the bumpy shuttle van ride, the choppy ferry ride. I dig deep for a cheery smile, throw my smaller bag over my shoulder, pull my suitcase from the hold.

I yank the handle to its full length and look down at my black rolling suitcase. A heavy sprinkling of white powder now dusts the top and one side. It looks like baby powder. Lots of it. As if to reinforce the theme, there's also a wipe tied to my luggage tag. Before I left my house, I'd forgotten to attach a brightly colored ribbon so I'd be able to distinguish my black rolling suitcase from the zillion other identical black rolling suitcases. So when my husband pulled up to the curb to drop me off at the Atlanta airport, I found a dried-up packet of wipes in the glove compartment, tore one in half vertically, and tied it to the handle.

I know I'm overreacting, but my suitcase makes me feel like a loser, like I've arrived at a hip cocktail party wearing a box of Pampers over my head. Or as if I'm still trying to pass for a suburban swim mom even though my youngest child is twenty-seven. I'm swept down the ramp with the other passengers and head toward two women, one holding a sign with my name on it. I manage not to throw up on them when we introduce ourselves and hug. But in my worst knee-jerk fashion, I start apologizing about my suitcase and telling them I have no idea where all that white stuff came from.

Janeen's mother, Mary, looks my suitcase, and me, up and down. "Cocaine?" she says.

This may or may not be an upgrade to my image, but I'll take it. I love both women immediately—their vibrancy, their colorful clothes, their friendliness. Mary watches my powdered suitcase, while Janna takes me across the street to the bank to help me get pesos from the ATM. Janna is thirty-three and already in full reinvention mode. She's opted out of her high-pressure public relations job in New York City as well as her high-rent apartment in Brooklyn to move to Isla Mujeres for the winter. She's blogging, dancing with a burlesque group, working with PR clients as well as for the conference.

"Wow," I say, "good for you."

"Thank you," she says, and I get the feeling she's a little bit relieved I didn't say, *Are you crazy?*

When I was thirty-three I had a five-year old daughter and a two-year-old son, a husband, two jobs, two dogs, one cat, a house—and I was more than a decade away from my own reinvention. I don't think Janna's timetable is better than mine was, or worse. Lots of roads will take you there. The important thing is that you go.

We grab a taxi. Mary and Janna take me to my hotel to check in. I'm tired and still a little bit queasy. What I really want to do is crash.

But I've promised myself that I'll be a full participant, so I throw my stuff into my hotel room, pausing only long enough to brush my teeth and hang up the clothes I need for tomorrow, since I'll speak first thing in the morning. And then we head off to the meet and greet.

As soon as we say hello, Janeen feels like a long lost friend, a kindred spirit. The party is breaking up when we get there, but Janeen invites me to dinner. The reservation is over an hour and a half away, and I know I'll be toast by then. So I join another group of women going off to eat. The whole thing feels effortless. I think about how cool it would be to be able to drift along like this always, opening my front door and joining forces with a bunch of women I've never met without even knowing where we'll end up.

As tired as I am, I realize almost immediately that I'd never, ever get any writing done.

REINVENTION INSPIRATION

If you haven't identified your reinvention destination yet, perhaps one of my fictional characters can help you. In each of my eleven novels, the heroine is stuck in some way and trying to find her own next chapter. I didn't really plan this common thread. It just happened organically because I find lives in transition fascinating and also, I think, because I always try to write the book I'd want to read.

There's nothing rarefied about the lives of these women. Just like the rest of us, they're trying to survive and thrive in these swiftly changing, crazy times, and that often boils down to reinvention.

Sarah in *Must Love Dogs* is a preschool teacher, and in Book 2, *Must Love Dogs: New Leash on Life*, she takes on a summer consulting gig teaching social skills to twenty-somethings at a video game company. In *The Wildwater Walking Club*, Noreen is duped by a sorta boyfriend into taking a corporate buyout and gets involved in walking and lavender and clotheslines. In *Life's a Beach*, Ginger transitions from a series of dead-end sales jobs to making sea glass jewelry while she spends time on a movie set as her nephew's guardian.

In *Summer Blowout*, the family business is a hair salon, and Bella's reinvention involves staying away from her ex-husband, who has run off with her half-sister, and creating her own personalized makeup kits. March and her daughter go to college at the same time in *Multiple Choice* and end up with their own radio show. Melanie in *Time Flies* is a metal sculptor with a highway driving phobia. Deirdre in *Wallflower in Bloom* is a social media maven and personal assistant to her famous brother. Beth in *Ready to Fall* collects quotes for a publisher. Sandy in *Best Staged Plans* is a home
stager, and Jill in *Seven Year Switch* is a cultural coach.

I love my heroines, and I've loved learning everything I could about the lives I've created for them, sometimes almost enough to want to jump off my own path and follow them. But in the end, nothing suits me better than writing my next book.

One of my favorite parts of being a novelist is that I get to live all of my heroines' lives vicariously, but still stay in my own wheelhouse, focused on the thing I do best. I log lots and lots of research hours as I'm writing each book, because I think those authentic details are crucial to the believability of a novel. By the time the book is finished, I've learned volumes about a whole new world I would have known nothing about otherwise. And then I move on to my next novel, and all my hard-earned knowledge fades away.

Maybe one of my heroines will help you find your reinvention destination and even give you a glimpse of the roadmap you'll need to get there. Or maybe simply reading through the list of their fictional jobs above will trigger something and send you in another direction.

SPEAKING OF DIRECTION, OR LACK THEREOF

I have a terrible sense of direction, so in my own reinvention, I just keep heading toward the light. This strategy turns out to be less effective in an actual place. Even though Isla Mujeres is a small island, less than five miles long by about half a mile wide, I'm all turned around and have no idea which direction my hotel is. I'm hoping one of the women in our dinner group is staying at the same hotel, so I don't have to try to find my way to it alone after we've finished eating.

I must not be the only one in my group who looks lost, because Tiffany Lanier, who is in charge of logistics for the conference, rounds us up and herds us over to her SUV. In 2002, Tiffany arranged her own reinvention by creating SunHorse Weddings, which has since planned over four hundred destination weddings on Isla Mujeres.

Tall Tiffany, as she is known because apparently there is a shorter Tiffany living on the island, loads us into her vehicle and drives us the very walkable distance to Hidalgo, a pedestrian-only street packed with restaurants. She opens the car doors and flips the back seats forward so we can all climb out. Then she points us in the right direction. Just to be on the safe side, she keeps pointing as we walk. She's both uber efficient and fun, and I can see why her business is so successful.

The group ends up choosing an Italian restaurant, which seems a bit random to me since we've just arrived in Mexico, but I go with the flow. We find seats at a long table overlooking the patio. Or maybe we're actually on the patio. With all the open air spaces, I'm finding it hard to distinguish inside from outside. Patios turn into cobbled streets, and there are so many restaurants so close together that one appears to morph into another. Strings of white lights are looped everywhere, echoing a sky twinkling with stars.

I'm too tired to actually count, but I think there are eight women at the table. A Catherine, a Katherine, Kathia, Corrine, Merlyn, some others whose names I don't quite catch. The menu offers selections in English as well as in Spanish, which is a good thing because my high school and college Spanish seemed to slip away the moment I stepped off the plane. A couple of the women start chatting comfortably in Spanish to our waitress.

"Hola," I say when it's my turn to order. That's it, I'm tapped out. I switch to English to order a pasta and asparagus dish.

The food is great and so is the company, an assortment of women from Tucson, Texas, Seattle, Toronto and more. I fall into conversation with Katherine

McLeod, who sits around the corner from me at the head of the table. Her day job goes right by me, but I'm fascinated by her background in improv and the fact that she has a blog called *Getting Up There*. She talks about True Colors, which draws heavily on the Myers-Briggs personality test and attempts to group and identify personality types by color. We've just met, but she tells me we're both blue-oranges. When I Google it later, I decide I might actually be an orange-blue, but she's close. I can't decide whether Katherine is really good or I'm really transparent. I also can't get Cyndi Lauper's song "True Colors" out of my head now.

The side conversations wind down and we're all one group again. One of the women asks about *Must Love Dogs*, what the movie experience was like, if I got to meet the actors, if I thought the movie did justice to the book. I answer that I'll be talking about it the next day, and I don't want to bore them to tears by making them listen to it twice. I can tell they'd rather hear it now, like some kind of exclusive sneak peek, but they let me off the hook.

Our waitress clumps us randomly into groups and brings each group a separate check. I'm not sure if this is to make things easier for us or for her. Katherine and I are in the same group, and it turns out we're both pathetic at pesos. We manage to count out enough for the bill, as if it's Monopoly money, and then try to figure out the tip. We know we're in over our heads so we leave extra in case we've guessed wrong. Evidently we overshoot our mark because our waitress follows us out of the restaurant, asking if we'll be back tomorrow. It feels good to have made her night.

When our group gets to the end of Hidalgo Street, I remember I have absolutely no idea where the hell my hotel is. I mangle the pronunciation as I ask if anyone else knows. Catherine points up and there it is, at six stories one of the highest buildings on the island. It's been right in front of my nose all along, and it will be visible from just about everywhere I'll be for the next few days, my own little North Star.

BREAK IT DOWN

It's helpful to have a North Star of sorts as you're reinventing your life, too. Whenever I start to feel lost, I focus on my daily pages and they pull me back on track.

When I'm writing a novel, I write two pages (Times New Roman, 12 point, double-spaced, single-sided) a day, seven days a week. Oh, *puh-lease*, you're probably thinking. Two paltry pages? *You* could write twenty pages at a single sitting with one hand tied behind your back.

Well, sure you could. I bet if you were really determined, you could wake up tomorrow and walk twenty miles, too. And then you'd limp around for the rest of the month, icing your shin splints, promising yourself that you'll get back to walking again one day. Soon. Really soon.

No matter what is or isn't happening in my life, I can write two pages a day. Consistently. Day in and day out. And at the end of five or six months, even factoring in a few inevitable *I just can't do it any more* meltdowns, I have the first draft of a book. Rinse.

Repeat. And that's why I'm now the author of eleven books. And counting.

Another advantage to this approach is that I'm essentially living in the book as I write it, thinking about it constantly, jotting things down all day long and when I wake up in the middle of the night. I often stop writing for the day before I'm tapped out. This means I have a place to start the next day, which takes some of the pressure off. Sometimes I quickly type a whole bunch of things I don't want to forget at the bottom of the page before I close the document. Sometimes I reach for the nearest notebook and scribble them there. But I try not to let myself actually write ahead, because I've found that, for me, that usually makes the next day's writing much harder.

The next morning, I reread and polish the pages I wrote the day before as a way to find my way into my characters' heads and voices again. I don't allow myself to go back any farther than that at this point, unless I have a specific reason to do so. If I went back to the beginning at the start of every writing day, my perfectionist streak would kick in, and I'd still be tweaking chapter one of my very first novel. My goal at this point is to push forward, because I can't make a book better if I haven't written it.

Instead of two pages a day, I know lots of writers who set a time quota. Two hours. Or four. Or twelve.

This wouldn't work for me, simply because I can't be trusted. I would cheat. I'd start with the best of intentions. I'd open the manuscript, type a sentence, delete it, type it again. Then I'd check email, do a little

bit of Internet "research," answer the phone, check
Facebook, throw in a load of laundry, have a snack,
check Twitter. And about fifteen minutes before my
writing time was up for the day, I'd write really fast,
trying to make up for what I hadn't done.

I have to paint myself into a corner. Not only do I
commit to two pages a day, seven days a week, but I
write the page numbers on a paper calendar when I
finish writing them. I know, way dorky, but it works.
Because I can tell beyond the shadow of a doubt that
yesterday I wrote pages 131 and 132, which means that
today I absolutely have to write pages 133 and 134.
Like most novelists, I have an active imagination, and
this, coupled with my fair share of self-destructive
tendencies, means that if I don't do this, I'm
thoroughly capable of convincing myself that I've
written my daily pages when I really haven't. Because
I've agonized over those pages so much it almost *feels*
like I've written them.

My deal with myself is that I'm not allowed to go to
sleep until my daily pages are written. Sometimes it's
relatively painless and I finish early and then move on
to the rest of the day. Sometimes it's not, and I find
myself sitting in my office at 11 P.M., just trying to live
through that second page so I can finally go to bed. It
gets ugly sometimes, but my pages get done.

So figure out your own version of my two pages a
day. Maybe you're more trustworthy than I am, so
devoting an hour or two a day to drafting the roadmap
to your reinvention will work for you. Perhaps doing
two concrete things a day to move you in the right

direction makes more sense. Or maybe you decide your first step is to register for an online class to give you some essential skills you need before you go any further.

If this is sounding way too loosey-goosey to you, you might feel your time would be better spent creating an action plan. Preferably with lots of bullet points. Or a Pinterest board, which for me would be total procrastination, but for you might be just the thing you need to move you forward. Go for it.

Whatever you decide your two pages a day will be, commit to it. Open your notebook and write it down. And either get a dorky calendar like I use, or make sure you build in some other measurable strategy for making yourself accountable along the way. Because trust me, some days will be harder than others. Some days you will want to cheat.

PLOTTERS AND PANTSERS

Novelists divide themselves into one of two camps: plotters and pantsers. Plotters plot. They outline. They might even know the way their book is going to end before they write the first word.

Pantsers wing it. I'm a dyed-in-the-wool pantser. Outlining would make me feel as if I were writing a term paper, which would take all the fun out of it. And if you're going to write fun novels, you should be allowed to have some fun doing it, right? And why go through all the blood, sweat and tears of writing a book if you already know how it's going to end?

Once upon a time, early in my career, I'm invited to be part of a panel of authors discussing literary vs. commercial fiction at a writers symposium that takes place at a hallowed Ivy League university. In case you haven't already guessed, I'm lumped in with the authors representing the commercial side. I'm fine with this, even though it's clearly intended to be the lesser label, and all these years later I can still remember the literary elitism that hangs in the air that day, thick as smoke.

When my turn comes, I tell my lifetime of procrastination to first book in my minivan story, watching my subject-verb agreement and trying not to snap my pink bubble gum too obviously. We move on to questions, and someone from the audience asks me to describe my writing process.

The answer I give that day is the same one I'd give now. When I write the first draft of a novel, I try not to think too much or try too hard, because when I do, my writing goes flat. I have a sense of who my main character is, and because my books are written in the first person, my entry point tends to be capturing my protagonist's voice. Then, because I'm essentially writing slice-of-life novels, I think about what makes the book begin today instead of another day. What does my main character want, and what has just gotten in her way? Once I find that little explosion, I have my jumping off point. The characters react to the explosion based on who they are, and these reactions create a ripple effect. I just keep following the ripples, staying true to my characters, weaving threads, building layer upon layer, and eventually I have the first draft of the novel.

"That's ridiculous," another author on the panel says into her microphone. "You can't write a book like that."

"Tell me what you really think," I say into mine.

A sizeable laugh from the audience keeps me from shutting down and/or getting defensive, and instead I ask her about her writing process. We go back and forth, the audience watching our volley like a Ping-Pong game. The other author admits that even though she starts with a thoroughly detailed outline, hitting all the major plot points, somewhere around page 160 or so, she usually runs out of outline and has to wing it from there. And I admit that even though the whole time I'm writing I pretend I don't know where I'm going, if I'm really honest, the more I get to know my characters, the more I do have a sense of it, and a teensy bit of an outline might just sort of form in my head.

So I'm not sure pantsers and plotters are quite as different from one another as we like to think we are. For a plotter, maybe an outline gives the illusion of security, like being wrapped in a warm blanket. For a pantser, not using an outline might provide more of an adrenaline rush, the exhilaration of a free fall. Either way will get you there, and it might come down to choosing the one that best suits your personality.

To justify my pantser preference, I used to quote Robert Frost's "No surprise for the writer, no surprise for the reader." As in, if a famous poet like Robert Frost said it, it must be true. But now I think the important takeaway from that quote is that, whatever your process, you have to stay open to the surprises that come along. As you write your book. As you reinvent your life.

If you're open, if you're responsive, then these surprises, the things that pop up out of the blue while you're on the road, can end up being some of the best parts. This is not the same thing as getting distracted and changing course. This is about scooping up the magic you find along the way and bringing it with you to your destination.

Had I not been open to surprises, there would have been no dogs in the original *Must Love Dogs.* My jumping off point for the novel was Sarah, a divorced preschool teacher from a big interfering family who's great at her job but can't get her love life together. I knew her bossy big sister would place a personal ad for her and that she'd show up for a date and the most embarrassing person in the world would be waiting for her with a single yellow rose: her dad.

So, I'm writing a conversation between Sarah and her sister Carol. They're discussing personal ads, and Sarah says something about how kids and dogs always know who's real and who's only pretending to be. Carol tells her we can't mention kids or you'll scare 'em all away. So, because dogs are less threatening to potential dates, *must love dogs* finds its way into the personal ad.

It sounded like a title, so I went with it. And with dogs in the title, it occurred to me that, *hmmm,* perhaps it might be nice to have a dog or two in the book. So a St. Bernard named Mother Teresa galloped in, followed by two shar pei/Lab-cross puppies named Wrinkles and Creases.

When the novel was published, readers and reviewers enjoyed the big Irish-American family, the classroom and dating scenes. I got tons of email from women (and a few good men) who said the novel gave them the courage to jump back into the dating world, and even to place their first personal ad. I heard from lots of teachers who recognized me as one of them.

But the dog thing was big. Dog lovers are a loyal and wonderful bunch and they helped make *Must Love*

Dogs a success. They talked up my novel and came to my events, often bringing their own dogs with them. I signed almost as many books to Fetch and Fido and Fifi as I did to humans.

I do love dogs, but I never planned that twist. And in all the books I've written since, it's been amazing how often a certain idea, or even a minor character, that came along as I was writing has ended up being one of everybody's favorite things in the book.

All by way of saying that, whatever your destination, don't be so focused on it that you miss the gems sparkling up at you along the way. Scoop them up. Use them.

THAT FINE LINE BETWEEN MUST LOVE AND HATE

Since *Must Love Dogs* was first optioned, rarely a day goes by that someone doesn't ask me—in person, via Facebook or Twitter or email—about the movie. How did it happen? What was the experience like? Did you get to meet the actors? How cute was John Cusack, and by the way, do you happen to know if he's still single?

In the beginning, I was simply grateful. The *Must Love Dogs* movie was a ridiculously fun, mind-blowing experience that made my life about a zillion times more interesting. Even my two then-teenage kids thought I was cool for a week or two.

Eventually I moved on, but it seemed that nobody else quite did. I wrote another novel, and then another, and another. I put everything I had into them, trying to learn and grow and become a better writer with each one.

One of my new novels was chosen as a summer book pick by *Good Morning America*. Three of them made it into *People* magazine. *Good Housekeeping* called my writing "laugh out loud" and *Redbook* "gleefully quirky." The *Today* show featured me as a "*Today*'s Woman." I was a judge for the *Family Circle* magazine fiction contest, a finalist for the Thurber Prize for American Humor. I spoke and gave keynotes at festivals and conferences from New Orleans to Denmark. My books were translated into fourteen languages.

And all anyone wanted to talk to me about was *Must Love Dogs*. "Do you ever think you'll write another book?" someone would invariably say to me at a cocktail party as if I'd only written one book, just days after my fifth, or seventh, or tenth had been released. My publisher would land me an interview on one of the network affiliates to talk about my new book, and behind me on the TV screen they'd flash a larger than life cover of *Must Love Dogs*, my new book jacket nowhere to be seen.

I felt like a one-trick pony. Maybe even a one-trick puppy. And the worst part was that it seemed as if most of the people who wanted to hear every last detail about *Must Love Dogs* hadn't even read the book. They'd only seen the movie.

One day I was whining about this on the phone to the agent who represented my film rights at the time, and she said, "Claire, that's a star problem."

That was my wake-up call. Not that I think for one moment that I'm a star, but how lucky am I to have a problem like this? I mean, poor former swim mom and teacher, poor midlife author, one of her books was made into a movie and people still want to hear about it.

It's embarrassing to admit that I once felt this way, but I'm happy to report I'm over it. *Must Love Dogs* is the biggest gift of my career thus far, the gift that keeps on giving. It still plays all the time on television, and the DVD has been bundled with classic romantic comedies like *You've Got Mail.* The movie has a cult following, people who watch it over and over, often with their dogs.

And sure, lots of these people may never notice, or care, that the movie is based on a book, but lots more will discover the novel because of the movie. And if they like it, they'll want to read the rest of my books, because that's what readers do.

So the whole thing has a massively bigger upside than downside. And now when I receive a lovely review like this one in Shelf Awareness for my eleventh novel—"Claire Cook (*Must Love Dogs*) has built a brand writing light-hearted women's fiction blending kernels of the absurd and comedic in compulsively readable combinations"—I see the reference as a positive thing. *Must Love Dogs* is my identifier.

So I will absolutely share some *Must Love Dogs* stories as we move along, because they're fun and I'm lucky enough to have them to tell. And also because the experience taught me some good reinvention lessons, and my hope is they might help you out as well.

FLIP-FLOPPING

I wake up early the next morning and figure I've got some time to wander the streets of Isla Mujeres before I shower and get ready to speak. I brew a cup of the Trader Joe's coffee I brought with me while I pull on a T-shirt and yoga pants and lace up my sneakers. I tilt my head as I look through the expanse of glass at one end of my room so I can see the palm trees and white sand and endless blue-green water. It's the kind of vista a hotel would call *water view*, but minus the spin would be more accurately described as *water peek*. It's enough.

When I grab my room key and head out the door, the real view stops me. It's spectacular. I'm standing on the fifth floor outdoor walkway peering out over the rooftops and palm trees. Ocean and sky go on forever. And the light—there is nothing like the light by the sea. It's odd that the best view has been saved for the wide corridor leading to the rooms, but I have to admit it sure makes coming and going pleasant.

The woman at the front desk greets me when I get to the tiny lobby. "*Hola. Buenos días.*"

"*Hola. Buenos días,*" I repeat. Cool. My Spanish vocabulary is increasing exponentially.

The streets are virtually unrecognizable from the night before. Tables and chairs have been moved inside the restaurants, corrugated metal garage-like doors I hadn't even noticed pulled down to the ground. I find Hidalgo Street and stop for a quick breakfast at Rooster Café. Then I set off at a pretty good clip, taking a right at a huge statue of a guy holding a bottle of tequila because I hope it will be a can't-miss landmark when I work my way back.

I stop to take a photo of a family's worth of laundry hanging on a clothesline up on a tiny roof. It makes me think of my novel *The Wildwater Walking Club*. I can almost picture Noreen, Rosie, and Tess walking with me now. Around the corner I take a picture of a sun-bleached sign high up on another building that says LAUNDRY SERVICE/LAVENDERIA. I've already been considering writing another adventure for these characters, and these sightings feel like an omen. I think my fictional friends would like it here.

I walk some more, stop to take a picture of a chipped stucco wall covered with deep red bougainvillea in full bloom, another one of pink and yellow calla lilies flowering happily in spattered five-gallon paint buckets on the sidewalk.

I realize I'll never get a workout in if I don't stop taking pictures, so I swing my arms and try to concentrate on walking. Though it's nowhere near as hot as it will be in a few hours, I'm dripping with sweat already. My fitness focus lasts for maybe half a block, until I see a totem pole of sorts in front of a building with faded aquamarine wooden steps reaching up to a scratched red wall. The entire pole, or post, is completely covered with flip-flops that range in color from green to orange to pink to blue to black. Child-size flip-flops peek out adorably between full-size versions.

I make myself walk past the totem pole and turn the corner, but the whole time I'm striding along the waterfront, I'm thinking about how much I want a flip-flop totem pole outside my own house. Or maybe in my office. Why didn't I think to save all my kids' flip-flops as they outgrew them?

When I was on book tour for my novel *Life's a Beach*, flip-flops were my life. I did flip-flop giveaways. Readers decorated flip-flops with crazy creative things and wore them to my events. I even accumulated an entire wardrobe of jeweled flip-flops and flip-flop jewelry—all gifts from my amazing readers.

How had I missed flip-flop totem poles?

I check my watch and realize I'm in danger of missing my own keynote if I don't hurry. I turn around and retrace my steps as quickly as I can, then decide I have to stop and take a quick picture of the totem pole anyway, in case I can't find it again. Just as I have the shot lined up, I notice a man sitting in a chair on the porch a few feet behind the totem pole.

I don't know how to say "oops" in Spanish so I say it in English.

"It's okay," the man says as he smiles and nods. "All the gringos take that picture."

I take my gringo picture. I thank him and race back to my hotel room.

ROADBLOCKS

Let's start considering the roadblocks to your reinvention—which ones you'll scale, which ones you'll thrust out of your way like Wonder Woman, which you'll circumnavigate, and which are simply, or more complicatedly, the products of your own imagination.

I know what my own roadblocks were, and are, but on the off chance that I might have inadvertently skipped some self-sabotage possibilities, I decide to get more input. In one of the many joys of conducting research as a novelist, as opposed to, say, a scientist, I post on my Facebook author page: *Research question for my next book: What would you like your life to be in five years, and what's standing in your way?*

I love the women who hang out on my Facebook author page. They feel so much like friends that I often can't remember whether or not we've actually met in real life. Or maybe the Internet and social networking have changed my definition of real life. Once again, they don't let me down. The responses just keep coming, and I'm fascinated by and grateful for each and every one of them.

It doesn't take long to see that, when it comes to obstacles, we have a theme. *Money. My mortgage. Money or lack thereof. Lack of money. Money. Money/benefits. Bills and money. College loans. Cost of living. The hefty price tag. Finances. Money. Money. Money. Money.*

I get it. Boyohboy, do I get it. And now I can't get Pink Floyd's "Money" out of my head.

If your reinvention destination is anything like mine, the money part will always be a challenge. People often ask me why I'm still driving my old Honda Element (Um, it still runs?) instead of maybe a Jaguar, and I can't tell you how many times I've been hit up for loans and even a "sponsorship." While I still love my Element, I actually wouldn't mind finding one of those sponsorships myself.

I'm not crying poverty. As one of eight kids who survived a rough childhood, I know the difference. There have been times in my career as a novelist when I've felt insanely lucky to have so much moolah, almost temporarily rich. But once I factor in taxes and quarterly estimates and agency commissions and paying my own health insurance and wondering if I can do it all again with the next book, uncertainty changes everything. Sometimes I even miss my old teacher paycheck—it wasn't much, but my bills and I could count on it coming on the 1st and 15th of every month.

One of the toughest things about being a novelist is that for almost fourteen years I've never known when the next check will arrive. I've signed a contract. I know the payments will come in four installments: on signing, on approval of the finished manuscript, on release of the hardcover, on release of the paperback.

Sounds pretty straightforward, right? Well, that first check for signing might take three months, or longer, to show up on my doorstep to help pay some bills. Publisher and literary agency have to agree on every last detail of the wording, then the check has to go to the agency, which takes its percentage and cuts me a check for the rest. Sometimes the timing works.

To further complicate things, it's been impossible to accurately estimate my earnings from year to year to make my required quarterly payments to the IRS. Foreign sales, audio sales and film options are all unknowns. Sometimes my guestimate is pretty close.

But one year, I will never, ever forget my stress level ramping up as I watched April 15th loom ever closer. A substantial signing check on a new two-book deal with a big New York publisher was on the way and should have arrived months before. I'd had a great year the year before, so my husband and I had paid off debt and tucked every cent we could into retirement. But unfortunately, that great year meant I'd guestimated low on my quarterly payments, so now I owed Uncle Sam a big chunk of tax money, which the check would take care of, no problem.

The perfect storm was brewing. If the check didn't arrive in time, I couldn't pay what I owed, and I couldn't access any other funds without paying a penalty.

The check didn't arrive in time.

I'm embarrassed to say it, but that year we paid our taxes with a credit card, which everybody, including our accountant, will tell you is the stupidest thing you can do, because the IRS hits you with a pretty big fee for credit card payment.

But we did it anyway because, short of a sponsorship, we didn't have another option. And the next week, the very next week, my signing check arrived.

My point? Don't quit your day gig.

Especially in the beginning. Oh, the pressure. The pressure. It would have derailed me if I'd quit teaching and knew I had to make a certain amount of money as a novelist by a certain time to pay my bills.

But, you say, if I can't quit my day job, how can I manage to reinvent my life?

You acknowledge how hard it's going to be. You decide you want it enough to do it anyway. You get determined. You get disciplined. You get tenacious. You give up some sleep, television time, any semblance of a social life, at least for a while. You find pockets of time in your existing life that you didn't even think existed.

When I wrote my first novel in my minivan in the parking lot in the wee hours of the morning outside my daughter's swim practice, it wasn't because it would make a good suburban mom-turned-writer story to tell for the rest of my career. It was simply all the time I had.

I was a teacher at one school and I consulted for two others. My daughter swam six days a week, twice a day on five of them. My son was involved in karate and soccer. My husband was a land surveyor, and as much as he would have loved to spend every waking moment with our kids, if he didn't show up for work, he didn't get paid.

It was the busiest time of my life. My only window for reinvention was 5:30-6:45 A.M. It was brutal. But I did it anyway.

One frigid morning that winter: I'm sitting in my minivan in the pool parking lot, trying to write fast enough to keep my fingers from getting frostbite. The heat is blasting and I've got the engine running so I don't kill the battery. Frost is forming so quickly on the windshield that it looks like icy stained glass, and I know I'll have to scrape the windshield again before I can drive home.

Suddenly, inches away from my head, there's a sharp knock-knock-knock on the driver's side window.

I jump, crashing my head so hard against the window I can almost feel it all these years later.

The windows are all fogged up and I can't see out, so I click the doors locked and lower my window a careful couple inches.

An elderly man wearing a snow-dappled hat and scarf peers into my car. He blinks a few times. "Are you all right?" he asks.

"Hanging in there," I say, thinking we are engaging in some kind of New England winter weather conversation. "How 'bout you?"

"I thought you were trying to kill yourself," he says.

After dropping off my daughter, I'd driven to the far, deserted end of the parking lot to hide out and write. My engine has been running for almost an hour. It's still insanely early in the morning.

"I'm fine," I say, "but thank you for caring enough to check."

He gives me a wave that's half salute, and then he turns and walks away. After he disappears from sight, I still hear the dry crunch of his boots in the snow.

I leave my window open a crack to be on the safe side and make a mental note to check my exhaust pipe for obstructions tomorrow morning before I start writing. It would really suck to accidentally kill myself before I finish this book.

Some of those mornings that winter were agonizing. Writing my first book while trying to juggle all the rest of the balls of my life was exhausting. But I have to say it never got so bad that I even once considered killing myself on purpose.

Hang onto that. And check your exhaust pipe.

HAIR TODAY

After a quick shower, I work a handful of styling mousse into my hair. This trip to Isla Mujeres is one of the first times I've been out of my house in over three months without a knit hat over my head.

I never planned to have a hair reinvention. But my hair had other ideas. I'd been getting it dyed to cover the gray for so long I could no longer remember exactly when I started. The grayer it got, the greater the contrast became between the color it wanted to be (white) and the color I wanted it to be (brown).

Because my hair grows quickly, I'd have about two and a half good weeks after a dye job, and then the ever-widening skunk stripe would start to emerge. This didn't bother me so much if I was home in my pajamas working on a book, but when I was in book tour or speaking mode, skunk wasn't the look I was going for.

Like many women, I spent way too much time trying to figure out the most strategic time to book my color appointments so I'd be root-free when it counted. Not only was this not the life I aspired to, but my hair seemed to be over it, too. It was getting increasingly resistant to dye. So my hair stylist would add more accelerant, or wrap my head in foil or a shower cap, or put me under a steam machine. I'd sit with the dye glopped on my head longer. And longer. And longer.

Finally I was up to fifty minutes. Fifty minutes sitting on my butt in a hair salon checking email or flipping through magazines. Every three or four weeks, give or take. Not only was it a crazy waste of time and expensive, but after all that sitting, I'd get home and still find tiny patches of pale hair where the dye hadn't taken.

A friend of mine, blond by choice as opposed to birth, once said that she hoped never to find out what her real hair color was now. I was actually kind of curious. One of my grandmothers had had gorgeous, thick white wavy hair, and I wondered if somewhere under all this hair dye, I might have gotten lucky.

One day I ask my hair stylist, Katie, what it would look like if she bleached off all the dye. She says my hair would turn yellow, and not a good yellow. I ask what my options are for going au natural, and she says she could start adding gray highlights to my dark hair and brown lowlights to my graying regrowth. This wouldn't completely mask the transition, which would take a long time and might not look all that great while it's in progress, but eventually I'd get there.

"Or," she says, "you can just suck it up and look really bad for about twelve weeks, and then get a super short cut."

"Like a crew cut?" I say.

She shrugs.

So I start to watch my calendar for a three-month window without book or speaking events, and maybe a year later I find one, on either side of Christmas. This means saying no to a few holiday parties I can't imagine attending in a knit hat, or even the Santa hat I consider briefly, but that seems a small price to pay to jump off the vicious dye cycle.

As my multi-colored roots grow, I find it harder and harder to leave the house, even in my knit hat. I'm not overly vain, but I've seen those women with endless gray roots at the grocery store, and I'm not sure my self-esteem can handle being one of them. So far the good news is that I'm escaping all that hair coloring, but the bad news is that I might be on my way to becoming agoraphobic.

Katie goes off to have a baby, so twelve long weeks after my last dye job I track down a new hair stylist and make an appointment for my crew cut.

I show up to meet this perfect stranger with a skunk stripe a mile wide.

"Just cut it all off," I say. "Please."

"Wait," my new hair stylist, whose name is Rhonda Johnson, says. "Let's do the cut first, then see what we've got. We can always go shorter."

So she gives me a stylish, short cut. And when she's finished, my hair is sort of dark and light with dark tips, almost like it's supposed to look this way. Practically intentional. Dare I say *ombre*?

Rhonda holds up a mirror so I can see the back. "It looks great," she proclaims. "I would have done this on purpose."

So relieved not to be wearing a knit hat, I stop at a store on my way home to give my hair a test drive. Two hip-looking female twenty-somethings come up to me almost immediately. "I love your hair," one of them says.

"Very cool," the other one says. "My mother would never do that."

And that's how it goes. Younger women (and a few gay men) stop me to say they love my hair, and some women my age look at me like they'd never do that. But others stop me to tell me how brave I am and say they'd like to try it, too, if only they dared.

I see glimpses of my grandmother's beautiful white hair, and some cool salt and pepper stuff going on, too. And not to make too big a deal of it, but my hair reinvention makes me feel brave and liberated, like a midlife rebel. I realize that what I'm really trying to do is figure out how to own my real hair and age. How to look and feel sassy, yet classy, as I rock on down the road through one of my favorite stages of life so far.

In the ultimate test, I post a picture of my new do on my Facebook page. An avalanche of likes and posts follow. The incredible outpouring of kindness and encouragement makes every minute I spent under that ridiculous knit hat worthwhile.

I decide I'm going to use the dye-free time and money I've freed up to have some fun. As soon as I finish this book.

RISE ABOVE THE NEGATIVITY

When I first began speaking in front of groups, I'd get nervous. My voice would shake. My hands would tremble. I wouldn't remember to breathe. I'd forget what I was saying.

I still forget what I'm saying sometimes, usually in the middle of a sentence. Whatever. I just laugh and shake it off. But the other symptoms went away as soon as I realized that, like most of life, me being up on stage isn't really about me. It's about the people who took time out of their busy lives to come hear me. My job is to try to give everyone in the room what they came to get.

So I watch faces. I look for smiles and nods of recognition. Pantser that I am, instead of reading from notes or memorizing a talk, I shape it as I go along, as I attempt to read the room.

The We Move Forward participants who fill the big round gathering room instead of skipping off to the beach on this gorgeous sunny day are the perfect audience. They make eye contact, smile, nod, lean forward in their chairs.

They're seekers, I realize. That's what brought them to this conference. Whatever they're looking for—adventure, connection, a new chapter—I hope I'm able to share something they can take with them on their journeys.

One of the biggest pieces of advice I have to give, at the conference and in this book, is to rise above the negativity. After I wrote my first novel, people told me you couldn't get published without connections. I didn't know a soul and I got published. People told me my novels would never be optioned for film, because the romantic comedy was dead. I can't speak to the state of the romantic comedy, but three of my novels have been optioned to date.

Long shots happen every day. Believe in them. Believe in yourself. And rise above the people who are trying to hold you down.

I think sometimes this negativity is a misguided, ham-handed attempt at protecting you. For your own good. So you don't get hurt.

But scratch the surface and what might be going on is that you've stepped out of the box, and everybody around you is still in it. And sometimes, even though it's not at all your intention, you remind people of what they're not doing in their own lives.

When my new career began to take off, there were people in my life who couldn't handle it. I didn't see it coming—I was completely blindsided. It had never once occurred to me that everyone I knew wouldn't be happy for me. Ecstatic even. I think part of the reason it threw me so much was that I couldn't imagine not being happy for these same people if the tables had been turned.

I don't believe success has a scarcity element. Another person's success doesn't mean yours is less likely to happen. If everybody's reading your book, it doesn't mean they're not going to read mine. Readers read—not only one book but lots of books. Foodies eat, and not only at one restaurant. Fashionistas shop, and then they go to the next boutique and shop some more.

I used to think if I just tried harder, just gave someone some more attention, just downplayed the good things that were happening for me, I could salvage things between us.

It doesn't work. If a friend can't be happy for you, she's no longer a friend. Let her go. You'll end up with new friends, friends who get it. If it's a family member you can't cut loose, shrug it off, protect yourself, know that it's not you.

This negative energy can come from strangers, too. Once I gave the keynote at a book festival. It took place on a riverboat as part of a big fundraising luncheon. As I came to the podium to speak, most of the plates had been cleared and people were sipping coffee. It was another great, responsive audience, and I was having a blast.

Until I noticed that one woman, another author appearing at the festival, was still eating away. Not just eating, but chowing down, sawing a piece of chicken loudly with her knife, stabbing her plate with her fork, stretching across the table for the final roll left in the basket. Standing up again to reach for some sugar packets, bunching about five of them together and tearing off the tops. Yawning. Checking her phone.

She never once glanced up at me, not a single time, even though I was talking into a microphone directly in front of her.

It was really throwing me. Was I that boring? Was my talk somehow off the mark? Was I invisible?

And then it hit me. She wanted to be standing where I was, and she was really pissed off that she wasn't.

I don't think this woman was consciously trying to sabotage my talk, but I almost let her do it anyway. I was in a room full of lovely, attentive people, and all I was feeling were the bad vibes coming at me from one ill-mannered author.

I made a point of going up to her afterward to introduce myself and to say how much I looked forward to hearing her speak later in the festival.

She glared at me and said, "The work I did in the early eighties made your books possible."

Huh? A series of pithy responses found their way to the tip of my tongue, but I swallowed them back. I thanked her for making my work possible and made a quick getaway.

Jealousy is toxic. The best thing you can do is to blow it off and go find someone more pleasant to hang out with. And to make a vow to never, ever behave that way to another person.

Today, in this tall, circular room on Isla Mujeres, the light streams in from high windows with spectacular ocean views, and I see only kind-hearted, encouraging women. Sometimes you get lucky, or maybe that's simply the type of woman a conference like this attracts.

But there will always be people who will tell you why you can't do whatever it is you want to do. Ignore them and do it anyway.

There will always be critics, people who would rather disparage another person's hard work than roll up their sleeves and get to work themselves. Their numbers will increase as your star rises. Don't fight back, even if the other person threw the first rock, because if you do, then you're one of them. Ignore it and move on.

Often the negativity will come from within, in the form of self-doubt or fear or insecurity or the need for approval, and you'll be the person who's standing in your own way, as I have stood in mine so many times.

Sometimes I think dealing with the negativity might be the biggest challenge of all. So channel your inner Girl Scout and be prepared. Learn how to rise above it as often and as quickly and as gracefully as you can, because it will save you a whole bunch of unnecessary pain and suffering.

DEFINING SADNESS

On a Saturday morning when I am almost eleven, I knock at my best friend's front door.

"My mother died," I say when she opens it.

"No sir," she says, though since this is a Boston suburb, it sounds more like, "No, suh." Today, she would have said, "No way."

"Swear to gawd," I say. *Way.*

"Liar," she says. "You're making it up."

I'm not. The day before, my mother's flu had turned into sepsis. She slipped into a coma at the hospital and never came out, leaving five children under the age of twelve motherless. Neighbors met us in our driveway after school and brought us home with them. They didn't say much, but I knew my first pajama party, scheduled for that evening, was definitely canceled.

The funeral takes place on Valentine's Day, also my birthday. Back at the house, someone sticks candles on a dull chocolate cake, so unlike the heart-shaped, candy-studded pink ones my mother had baked for my other ten birthdays, and mourners sing "Happy Birthday" to me. After that, people start tucking bills— mostly ones and fives, and one hundred-dollar bill—

into the pocket of my dress, as if I were a prepubescent stripper-in-training. My mother would have found the whole thing incredibly tacky.

Over the years, I've met other women who lost their mom at an age when she was still the sun and the moon and their favorite hula hoop all rolled into one, yet they were also on the cusp of needing her to walk them through that first period and bra. Time heals most wounds, but not this one. Eventually, you learn to compartmentalize it, but this loss becomes the defining sadness of your life.

By the time I come out of my posttraumatic fog and really want to know what my mother was like—as a person, a woman, a friend—the people who could have told me about her are either dead or long gone.

Then one summer I have a book event near my mother's hometown on the other side of the state. A woman about my age, give or take, waits in line with an elderly lady in a wheelchair. The younger woman tells me her mother has something to say to me. I lean over the wheelchair and smile.

"Your mother was the most generous friend in the world. I went into labor with my son, Jimmy, in the middle of a blizzard," she says.

Even though it's a hot August night, a chill runs down my spine.

"The snow came so fast, my husband couldn't get home. I called the ambulance. I called the police. Nobody came. I called your mother. 'Put your coat on,' she said. 'It will be the adventure of a lifetime.'"

All these years later, sitting in her wheelchair, she giggles. "Your mother walked me all the way to the hospital in the snow, laughing and joking the whole time."

I reach out to hold her cool, dry hand, and it feels lighter than air.

"She was Jimmy's godmother, you know. Your mother had more godchildren than you could shake a stick at."

I'd been old enough to know my mother was big-hearted and smart and generous, to remember the huge pile of cards, with family photos tucked in, at Christmastime. But at that moment I feel her spirit again, as if it has lived on for decades in the heart of her friend, who is now bequeathing it to me.

My mother's death is still the defining sadness of my life, and though it's been many, many years since it happened, my eyes tear up as I type this. Her death is also the place my best writing comes from, even when I'm writing about other things. That raw place that will never heal over, the place that's so blindingly, painfully real that it triggers Technicolor images and feelings.

I think we all have that place. For me, at least, allowing myself to access it again after hiding from it for so many years has resulted in some of my best work.

TIME AND MONEY

According to the posts by my research colleagues over on my Facebook author page, money is the biggest obstacle standing in the way of reinvention. Time, or lack thereof, is right behind it.

Time. Kids and job. Long commute. Lack of time. Family obligations. Twin toddlers. Five-year-old live-in grandson. Waiting for retirement so have time. Hoping to win lottery. Need to win lottery. Waiting for inheritance. Hoping to take sabbatical. Time. No time. Time.

What I think is particularly interesting is the link between money and time. Even if, as The Beatles once proclaimed, money can't buy us love, it should at least be able to buy us time, right? If only I had X amount of money, I could quit my job/retire/hire a nanny/reach my dream.

I hear you. It's a great fantasy.

I have no idea whether or not nature really abhors a vacuum, as the old saying goes, but I do know that the moment some free time opens up in my own life, something else rushes in to fill it. So what I think might really happen if you won the lottery is that you might spend all the extra time that money freed up shopping for a yacht. If you came into an inheritance, you might spend it setting up a nanny cam to keep an eye on that new nanny you just hired. If it were me, I'm not sure a windfall would mean that I'd actually get my next book written any sooner than this one.

This is not to say I'm opposed to winning the lottery. In fact, I wouldn't mind a little lottery-winning action myself. But I don't think postponing your reinvention until you win it is a good game plan.

There was one more Facebook post about time that I thought was spot on, even though I'm pretty sure I'm not interpreting it the way it was intended: *Free time does not exist.* I think it might be a good idea to just accept the fact that free time will probably never happen in most of our lives. And then take all that wishing-and-hoping energy and reroute it in a more constructive direction.

Because even though free time might not exist, there are pockets of *unused* time in every life. Find them. Use them.

What I'm trying to say is that you don't have to leave your existing life to create a new one, at least in the beginning. In fact, doing so might generate a whole bunch of pressure you don't need. Picture quitting your job or taking a sabbatical or retiring and having hours and hours stretching out in front of you. Imagine completely unstructured days. Sounds heavenly, but it can really mess with your head when you finally have all the time in the world to do that thing you've been dreaming about your whole life. It can be hard to stay on track.

Winning the lottery would be a terrific problem to have, a genuine star problem. And if you're able to free up some time that way, or any other way, good for you.

If not, don't wait for it. It might even be an advantage if you don't have it. As I look back, I'm glad I had barely enough time to write my first book, and not all day to stress about it.

MORE REINVENTION INSPIRATION

One of the best things about being the kickoff speaker at We Move Forward is that I can now relax and enjoy the other speakers. They're all fascinating, each in her own way, and most of them have reinvented their lives.

Dina Francesca Haynes is one of the reinvention exceptions. As she puts it, "I've always been the seeker of justice." Dina is an international human rights lawyer specializing in women's rights. She's advised United Nations agencies as well as the White House on international women's issues. She talks about eradicating labor exploitation and tells us about representing the maids of diplomats in that class action suit I remember reading about. She speaks about human trafficking, and how hard it is to get attention for it unless it's sensationalized—as in women chained to beds in a brothel—which keeps us from seeing countless other women in need.

Dina shares one of my favorite Gloria Steinem quotes, "The truth will set you free. But first it will piss you off." She introduces me to my first Chad proverb,

"However long the night, the dawn will break." She's a force. She's humble. She's amazing. And suddenly I'm wondering what the hell I'm doing frittering my life away writing novels when I could have gone to law school. Is it too late?

But then Dina moves on to what she calls "food insecurity" and says that when women in war-torn places are asked, "What do you need?" the answer is consistently food. I realize that I can donate more food, even closer to home where I know poverty has also created plenty of food insecurity. I can help get the message out about donating food. I can still keep my day job.

"What can we do to help?" another woman in the audience asks.

"Create a welcoming and warm environment in your community for refugees," she says. "Xenophobia is a huge obstacle." I can look for ways to do that, too, maybe even find a way to sneak it into my next book. (Here it is!)

And then I remember that one of the first things Dina said in her opening comments was that she hadn't brought any of her own books with her, but she'd brought a copy of my novel *Life's a Beach*, which she was looking forward to reading on Isla Mujeres. At the time, I'd thought it was such a kind and generous thing to say, but now I realize there might be more. It didn't let me off the hook in terms of making other contributions, but if anybody in the world needs a fun beachy book to escape to every once in a while, it's Dina Francesca Haynes.

BE WHO YOU REALLY ARE

Branding is the big buzzword these days, but I prefer to think of it as authenticity. Being a novelist is the first job I've ever had where I wasn't pretending, or at least trying to pretend, to be a slightly different person. If we were to meet at a women's conference or the grocery store or a Hollywood party or the pages of one of my books, I'd be exactly the same person. Who I am and what I write are totally in synch. There's tremendous power in that.

In my teaching days, I was always trying, though not very successfully, to dial it down a notch, to squelch my natural enthusiasm and rebelliousness so I'd fit in better with the other teachers. When I was running my own dance aerobics business back in the '80s, I remember being in the restroom at a training conference while an emaciated instructor stuck her finger down her throat behind a stall door and threw up the blueberry muffin she'd just wolfed down. Everybody else kept fluffing their big hair and adjusting their leg warmers and thong leotards like it was no big deal, but I remember thinking, *Holy body image issues, Batman.*

My next thought was, *I think I'm at the wrong conference.*

I was also such a people pleaser. Like me. Oh, please, like me. Wait, let me tweak this and then maybe you'll like me more. Let me spin what I'm really thinking so you'll like me even better.

Lots of women might come to it earlier, but for me, midlife brought the courage to change all that. By that point in my life I'd made just about every mistake you could make, embarrassed myself more ways than I ever would have thought possible.

A Robert Frost quote hangs on Meredith's bulletin board at work: "In three words I can sum up everything I've learned about life: it goes on." Meredith says, "It reminds me not to beat myself up when I make a mistake."

I managed to live through each blunder I made, and when I'd lived through enough of them, I lost the fear. So what if I try something and it doesn't work and it makes me look ridiculous. Been there a few hundred times. So what if I say something that everybody doesn't agree with. What else is new. Playing it safe gets you just about nowhere. Why not put my real, undisguised self out there and just go for it?

It's not that I don't still hope people like me. Of course I do. I think it's human nature, or at least my nature, to want that. But if they don't—oh, well. As Popeye sang, "I yam what I yam, and that's all that I yam."

After a lifetime of splashing away in all the wrong ponds, when I found the right pond I knew it almost immediately. These new frogs thought like me, croaked my language. For the first time just being me was enough. My readers didn't want me to change. They just wanted more.

So if your existing life doesn't feel like a good fit, factor that in as you plan your reinvention. Instead of changing yourself to fit your life, you might want to think about finding a life to fit your self.

When Jenny's career with a big pharmaceutical company was no longer feeling like a fit, she took a buyout and started a blog called *Hated My Job. Left. Now What?* to help her through the transition. "I didn't know what I wanted to do. I only knew I couldn't keep doing what I had been doing. I was done with the corporate world. When I realized that I could financially manage going to grad school, it opened a world of possibilities."

In her research, Jenny came across programs that combined environmental science with policy. She applied and received several offers. At the same time, she started volunteering in wildlife rehabilitation and fell in love. She sold her house and packed up and moved to attend the school she'd chosen. It was a long, tough road, but she eventually got a job as a seasonal clinic supervisor at a bird rescue and research center. "I never in a million years thought I'd ever actually get paid to work with wildlife," Jenny says. "Dreams can come true!"

In my own reinvention, I've also learned that I don't have to write everybody's books, just mine. My gift as a novelist is to make people laugh. And to recognize themselves and their quirky friends and families and maybe feel a little bit better about their crazy lives. I read widely and voraciously, but as a writer I play to my strengths. I understand people, so my novels are character driven. I'm a huge eavesdropper—if you ever see me at a restaurant, I am soooo listening to the conversation at your table—which has taught me to write dialog that rings true.

I'm writing for my readers, the ones who get it, the ones who like my novels, the ones who cheer me on and can't wait for my next book. I don't change what I'm writing to try to appeal to the people who *don't* like my books. If my books aren't their cup of words, I wish them well. I hope they find another book they'll be happy with. But if I were to change my books to try to appeal to every single reader in the whole wide world, I'd probably lose all of them. I'd certainly lose the things that make my writing special. I'd lose myself.

Call it brand or niche or authenticity, but wherever you're going in your reinvention, I think it's key. What makes what you're doing so *you* that people can find you in the midst of all the deafening noise going on around us? My novels are rarely compared to those of other authors. My voice is uniquely mine, as are my stories. This doesn't mean you're necessarily going to like a Claire Cook book, but if you do, you'll know you can come back for more.

You may not like the Etsy shop that sells shelves made of recycled plumbing parts, but you're certainly not going to confuse it with the other shops. I recently hired a floor company to repair our bamboo floors because the woman who owns it has this huge graphic of a '50s housewife painted on the side of her vans. I didn't even quite get the point, but it was so unique that it drew me in enough to find out more. I chose my new hair stylist because her website made her seem like a real person who knew what she was doing.

As Oscar Wilde said, "Be yourself; everyone else is already taken." Whatever your reinvention goal, think about who you really are and what unique qualities only you can bring to it. These qualities might even be things you're so close to you have to step back in order to see them.

When I first started working with the editor of one of my early books, we were chatting on the phone and she said something along the lines of, "These Irish people are terrific." And I'm thinking, *There are Irish people in my book?* I had absolutely no idea. Or at least I'd never really thought about it that way.

But I'd lived for most of my life on the South Shore of Boston, an area that's frequently referred to as the Irish Riviera. According to an article that's been floating around on the Internet forever, Scituate, the town I lived in, holds the record for having the biggest Irish population in the United States.

So, essentially, even if you're not Irish when you first move in (though I am, as well as part English and Scottish), it wouldn't take you long to pick up the vibe. Big hearts. Big families. Big mouths. Great stories. Flip, wicked funny senses of humor. And I knew from being part of a big family that it's like playing that old game of telephone—by the time I say something to my sister in Rhode Island and it goes to my sister in Georgia to my brother in Pennsylvania to my brother in Louisiana to my sister in Massachusetts to my brother in California to my other sister in Georgia and back to me, it's a whole new animal. And I swear I never said any of it.

I've received lots of email from readers who've written to tell me that their family is just like one of my fictional families, but they're Southern Baptist or Polish, and then they go on to tell me a crazy thing that just happened. So it's not about the religion, even though the specific details might be. It's not about the ethnicity. It's about the authenticity. And it can be so much a part of your normal that sometimes you can't even see how unique and valuable it is.

That inside track can be something you're embarrassed about or have been devastated by, something you'd just as soon leave in the dust, thank you very much.

You ran off with your sister's boyfriend when you were sixteen, you're dealing with a rare disease, you're massively computer phobic, you've lost a ton of weight and then gained back two tons, you left an abusive marriage in the middle of the night.

A writer I know was having a hard time selling her first novel. When I heard her describe it, it sounded a bit too familiar, like something I'd read many times before. I knew this writer well enough to know she had a son who struggled with major health issues. She'd turned her life upside down to support him, and she was passionate about helping other families in similar situations. She knew the emotions of that struggle in a way you couldn't possibly know them unless you'd been there.

I asked her why she wasn't writing about that instead, or at least weaving a thread about it through her novel, which I thought might make the book feel fresh and also deepen it.

"I have to live through it," she said. "I don't want to have to write about it. I want to write fun books."

I see her point. And yet, I think tapping into these places of pain can lead to powerful reinventions.

A woman who came to one of my first reinvention workshops, inspired by the struggles of a loved one, created a claw-like gadget to help physically handicapped people reach things on upper shelves, as well as a long-handled shoehorn to enable them to slide their feet into their shoes independently.

Katrina, an internal auditor with lots of acronyms after her name—CPA, CFE, CFF, CIA—spends most of her working hours figuring out who is stealing from their place of employment. Because of that, Katrina felt she was turning into a negative, cynical person and she didn't like it. So, without giving up her first profession, she also became a certified health coach to balance it. (I hope she offers a twofer discount if you book both services!) Such a brilliant way to reinvent your life without leaving it.

Candace Hammond was married at twenty. She suffered from debilitating panic attacks and became agoraphobic. When she was forty, her "safe person"—her husband—left her and Candy was forced to face her fears and "push myself back out into the world." Seventeen years later, she's a journalist and appears on radio and television. She also performs live with her cowriter of *The Fix-It Sisters*, a humorous column that will soon be nationally syndicated by Gatehouse Media-owned newspaper websites.

Some of the speakers at the We Move Forward conference have turned painful experiences into reinvention. When Mary Carwile was fifty-five, with breast cancer and two divorces behind her and her world shrinking, she reinvented herself by becoming a flight attendant, even though she was claustrophobic and terrified of flying. She went on to reinvent herself again as a motivational speaker. Dressed in her uniform and holding up an oxygen mask, she takes the safety spiel we've heard so many times at the beginning of our flights and turns it on its head until it's a metaphor for living our best lives. She finishes by passing out airline wings pins to all the women in the audience and encouraging us to fly.

Miriam Laundry was in the hospital after giving birth to one of her four children when she got the word that her seventeen-year-old niece had committed suicide. Miriam turned her pain into passion by writing a self-esteem building children's book called *I Can Believe in Myself* and doing school visits.

Just before he was to be married, Joyce Urzada's son was murdered in a random act of violence, a "sport killing." A year and a half later, after deciding to leave a long-troubled marriage, Joyce's sister was murdered by her own husband.

When she speaks to us at the We Move Forward conference, Joyce is sad and strong and vulnerable, and most of all determined to turn the knowledge she's gained through her unimaginable losses into something that can help the rest of us.

She tells us, "You never get over the loss of a loved one. You're lucky if you get through it." And yet, "Being happy is our objective in life. It's a cellular impulse to reach for the light."

Joyce gives the roomful of women direct advice on how to deal with people in our lives when they lose a loved one. Don't tell them how to grieve. ("I will not should on you. And don't should on me.") Simply say I'm sorry for your loss and give them a hug. Be physically present even if the grieving person doesn't talk. Write a letter to them, detailing the good times.

"Don't say, 'Let me know if I can help,'" Joyce instructs us. "Of course you can help. Just do it. And then follow up in two to three weeks."

My heart breaks for Joyce and all she's been through, but wow, I'm awed by the power she's created with her pain.

IN THE BEGINNING

Let's say you've chosen your reinvention destination. You've started charting your course. It's all so exciting you can't wait to tell everybody you know.

You might actually want to wait, at least for a while. It's not that I'm worried about somebody copying my work, or stealing my idea for the next book. Even if we all decided to write a book based on the same idea, our finished books would be completely different. And I think good ideas are everywhere, as long as your eyes and ears are open, and finding them can become the easiest part of it once you train yourself to start noticing them.

A few minutes ago: I'm at the grocery store. Tomorrow's a holiday and just about everybody in Metro Atlanta, including me, is here to pick up the essential items they'd forgotten to buy earlier in the week. Most of them are not happy campers.

I push my cart into one of the endless lines and get ready for a long, boring wait. Just as I start to drift into a daydream, the elderly woman in front of me throws both hands up in the air and announces that she forgot the crackers.

"Go," I say. "I'll watch your cart for you."

She dances over to an end cap display of crackers an aisle away from us. She's adorable—short, short see-through white hair, sweatpants with a perky vest and multicolored fluorescent sneakers. She picks up a box of crackers, jerks it high over her head, spins around with it, puts it back down, and repeats the whole thing with a different box. There's a big dash of *I Love Lucy* physical comedy in her moves.

"That's what's wrong with the world," she says, projecting her voice so that the front end of the grocery store can hear her. "There are far too many choices." She grabs another box of crackers and twirls around again, crackers way up in the air, her non-cracker-bearing arm extended gracefully.

It's almost her turn and I don't want to cut her performance short, so I start loading her groceries on to the belt for her.

"Bacon," she trills. "I mean, I ask you, who needs bacon in their crackers? The world was a far better place before we had to decide whether or not we wanted bacon in our crackers."

She hugs a box of bacon crackers to her chest. "They're good enough," she says as she dances back over to her place in line. "Actually, any of them would be good enough. I mean, think about it, they're crackers, not husbands."

The cashier starts to ring her order.

The bagger asks, "Paper or plastic?"

"I don't give a rat's ass," the woman answers and everyone within earshot cracks up, including the bagger.

I'm about to tell her she should think about doing stand-up comedy, but she's already moved on to coaching the cashier about her love life.

The woman is gone before I can ask her name, but just like that, I have the beginnings of a minor character for a future novel. As soon as I get my groceries to the car, I root around for a notebook in the chaos of my glove compartment.

Ideas might be everywhere, even, or maybe especially, at the grocery store. Putting your fresh spin on the one you choose and doing the hard work that follows are often the bigger challenges.

I've learned the hard way that talking about a project too early can open me up to several roadblocks. Say you decide you're going to start a business. You're so excited, you email everybody you know about it, and then you wake up the next morning with a major case of buyer's remorse. What a stupid idea. What was I *thinking*? But the truth is you don't know yet whether it's a good idea or not. Sit quietly with it for a while so you can hear yourself think as you let it incubate and grow. Do your initial research and planning before you start telling the world.

Also, when I'm starting a new book, I have to psyche myself up. I have to *believe* I can do it. I have to trust the process. I even try to visualize this perfectly formed and totally finished novel existing somewhere in a parallel universe, and all I have to do is capture it and reel it in. This may or may not be a total crock, but it gets me through those tough early stages until the book starts to take on a life of its own.

Because my book and I are really fragile at this point. I haven't figured out what I'm doing yet, and if I talk about it, this becomes more and more painfully apparent. And even eleven or twelve books in, I'm tempted to give up on the whole stupid writing thing and look for another teaching job. Worse, if I share my idea for the new book and everybody starts telling me why it can't or won't or might not work, this could really derail me.

Talking about a book that isn't written also drains some of the energy, some of the magic, away from it, and I start to feel that I've actually finished today's pages, when I haven't written word one. If words are coming out of my mouth, they're not coming out of my fingers.

This classic E. L. Doctorow quote says it all: "Planning to write is not writing. Outlining—researching—talking to people about what you're doing, none of that is writing. Writing is writing."

I think this can be applied to just about any new project. There will be plenty of time to seek support from the people in your world as well as to get that all-important outside advice. But everybody's got an opinion, which doesn't necessarily come hand-in-hand with knowledge, and in the beginning, I'm not sure that input is anything but potentially confusing. You're asking these people to picture something you haven't figured out yet, even for yourself, so any feedback you get will be based on their interpretation of your vagueness, which can send you bouncing all over the place.

I can remember really early on asking someone to critique the beginning of one of my novels. With the best of intentions, she got out her red pen and stripped my voice right out of it, changing even the punctuation. What was left when she finished was totally generic. I was developing my own writing style, and she didn't get it. Had I listened to her, I would have thrown away my uniqueness.

As Seth Godin said, "We do great work when we announce, not when we ask."

All by way of saying that, as you start to figure out your path, consider keeping it to yourself for a while. Put on your blinders and just place one foot in front of the other for the first leg of the journey.

LETTING GO

What do my Facebook posters want their lives to be in five years? Renae wants to be moved into a smaller home with a small lawn. "What's standing in my way, you ask? ME. My husband passed away and all his memories are in this house. Just can't make myself leave, feels like I am leaving him."

My heart breaks for Renae, and I would never presume to comment on her situation, other than to say I'm so, so sorry for your loss. What I do know personally is how hard it is to let go of a home you've lived in for twenty-one years.

My house story: Even though we knew only rich people should buy houses like this one, my husband Jake and I buy our equivalent of the house in the movie *The Money Pit* with our hearts and not our heads. It's an 1890 Victorian on an acre of land with a pie slice-shaped acre of lawn stretching out in front of it like an old New England town common in a beautiful beach town. It has mature perennial beds and huge stately conifers arranged in a half circle to shield it from the street.

The house has been on the market for two years without an offer, in part because it had been turned into The Voice in the Wilderness Pentecostal Church, a ministry for wayward boys. I don't know how many parishioners or wayward boys were ever collected, but ultimately they were unable to get tax-exempt status in Massachusetts, so they packed up and headed out, looking for greener pastures.

Our realtor tries to nudge us toward a garrison colonial on a cul-de-sac instead, but we keep dragging her back to this house. Our starter house, a three bedroom ranch with one bath, sells quickly, so we put in a lowball offer and it's accepted.

The former owners leave us a wooden pulpit in the living room and a sign over the fireplace that says REPENT. There are empty shotgun shells on the floor of the unfinished room over the garage, and reddish stains on the blue shag carpeting on the staircase leading up to the second floor that make us think at least one of the wayward boys had a good aim.

They also leave a mammoth, locked stainless steel restaurant freezer in the dining room. Since the utilities were cut off months ago for nonpayment of bills, this does not bode well. We walk close enough to get a good sniff and gag. We call restaurant supply people, offering to sell it cheaply, as is. They look, sniff, gag, and leave. We call professional cleaning services, who look, sniff, gag, and leave.

Finally we track down two guys who need Saturday night drinking money and pay them fifty bucks to haul the freezer to the dump. We're thrilled. They're thrilled, too, until they get to the dump and find out it's illegal to drop off a freezer without removing the doors first. It turns out the freezer is filled with rotting chicken. The stench causes a mass evacuation of the town dump.

But underneath the mess, and the flocked velvet wallpaper our kids grow up helping us peel from the walls, the house is gorgeous—ten foot ceilings, original moldings, original maple floors, original carved mahogany banister and mantel. We bring it back to its former glory and then some. When my father dies, we use my one-eighth share of the money he leaves for his children and not his third wife (forgotten IRA) and build Grandpa's Porch.

When our kids grow up and have pretty much flown the nest, Jake and I realize we rarely even set foot in half of the house, and we're still pouring an endless stream of money and elbow grease into it. Still, selling that house is one of the hardest things we've ever done.

Twenty-one years of things we'd thrown up in the attic or down in the basement, just in case, to sort through. Twenty-one years of high ceilings and beautiful moldings and the daylilies we'd collected to let go of. And those twenty-four Canadian hemlocks we'd planted to buffer the noise from First Parish Road. We'd bought them from long-gone Woolworth's for seven dollars each because that was all we could afford. And in twenty-one years they'd grown from pint-sized versions of Charlie Brown's Christmas tree into a towering hedge forty feet high.

The way I get through it is to write a novel with a heroine who is a home stager. While researching that world, I learn how to declutter and stage my own house. Even though the book isn't really autobiographical, lots of the little details are, and Sandy Sullivan's house in it is mostly my house.

Thanks to Sandy's staging expertise, our house sells in a tough market in two-and-a-half weeks. And *Library Journal* names *Best Staged Plans* one of the best women's fiction books of 2011. My husband and our dog Daisy and I move to Atlanta and create a new life, right down the street from our adult kids.

I still have all the memories. I can go through that 1890 Victorian in my mind and see every inch of it— the doorway where we marked our kids' height with a pencil, the chimney we exposed when we took down the wall between the kitchen and the front parlor. I can even open the kitchen cabinets in my imagination and pretty much remember what was in each one.

I can still see the pie-sliced front lawn where half the town of Scituate gathered every year in lawn chairs for the St. Patrick's Day parade, leaving cavernous tire marks in our wet spring lawn and everything from empty beer bottles to lollipop wrappers to, once, an unused condom in a green shamrock-stamped foil package, in their wake.

Two St. Patrick's Day parades have come and gone since we moved, and Jake and I high-five as we remember the crowd that's now in someone else's front yard. Our new house is simpler, which makes our life way easier and lots more fun. Our old friends are still in our lives, or at least on Facebook. When we miss the beach too much, we find one to visit.

Memories are portable. You can separate them from stuff and places and houses. You can pack them up and take them with you.

CONFOUND EXPECTATIONS

If everybody's doing it, it's already been done. This doesn't mean you shouldn't do it anyway, if it's a great idea. If you're passionate about it and it feels authentically you. Especially if it's your dream, or feels like it might just turn out to be what you want to be when you grow up.

But originality counts. Big time. So put a little surprise into everything you do. As Ralph Waldo Emerson once wrote, "Do not go where the path may lead, go instead where there is no path and leave a trail."

As The Cars once sang, "Shake it Up."

For instance, if I'm writing a novel about a midlife woman, I might give her a job that's totally out-of-the-box. She might have an unusual family. Unexpected obstacles will block her path. And if it looks like Y is going to happen, and it does, well, how boring is that. You could have just skipped the whole rest of the book. I've got to at least come up with a twist or two you didn't see coming.

ElizaJ.com is such an original idea that I wish I'd made it up for one of my heroines. Liza had spent many years in the events industry, and as she says, "Okay, almost everybody out there has experienced that dirty, disgusting, portable restroom at an outdoor event." So she started a company that rents classy portable restroom units. Some have solar-powered lighting and all have fresh water sinks, air-conditioning, air fresheners, and music. And they all come with amenity baskets filled with a combination of brand name and custom ElizaJ products, from stain remover to mouthwash. Plus fresh flowers. If you're still trying to figure out what's next for you, franchises are available!

You will never mix up Lisa Koch with anyone else. She's flown in from Seattle to perform at the We Move Forward conference. Her bio advises you to picture the triangulated love child of Bette Midler, Lily Tomlin, and Joan Jett, and goes on to describe her as an irreverent singer/comedian, out lesbian, and sober chick. Lisa plays the guitar and sings wickedly hilarious songs, some twisted mash-ups of classic rock songs, that capture all the quirky truths of being a woman: mammograms and midlife and hot flashes and love.

She's got a big message: acceptance—of self, of others and their differences, of same-sex marriage—but she manages to get it out there without being didactic, without even a hint of preachiness. While she's tuning a string on her guitar, she tells us that when you're laughing, a lot more info can come in because your heart is open. I think I've known that instinctively in my own career, but I've never thought about it that way, and hearing it from Lisa feels like a gift. I write it down so I won't ever forget it.

It also brings back a quote by Jean Houston that I love and haven't thought of in years: "At the height of laughter, the universe is flung into a kaleidoscope of new possibilities."

I haven't taken an actual poll, but I'm pretty sure that, other than her wife, Lynn, who's come with her, Lisa is the only lesbian in the room. But she is one of us immediately, or maybe it's one *with* us, and everybody adores her. As the We Move Forward audience cheers for Lisa, I wonder if it's too late for me to learn to play the guitar.

Throughout the rest of the conference, I notice women going up to Lisa to tell her that there were lesbians at last year's conference but they were the grouchy kind, or that their second cousin is also a lesbian. Finally, on the last night, I'm sitting with Lisa and Lynn and a group of other women, and I watch yet another woman come up to Lisa to tell her how much she likes Ellen DeGeneres.

I wait until the woman is out of earshot. "Does that ever bother you?" I ask. "You know, having everybody do that?"

She smiles. "I'm okay with it."

Lisa is just so authentically who she is, and she's mined her own life so deeply and creatively for her art, that it's really inspiring.

All by way of saying don't overlook the thing that only you could come up with. Own it. Milk it. Work it.

BIG MISTAKES
AND HAPPY ENDINGS

When the first publisher that asked to read my first novel wanted to buy it, I shouldn't have jumped so quickly. Back then, in the days before self-publishing lost its stigma and became a viable alternative, the big New York publishers were all-powerful. They were the gatekeepers, and you couldn't even get your manuscript in front of them without an agent.

I'd sent out exactly two query letters seeking representation to two agents, both famous enough that even I had heard of them. One never responded, but I heard from the other almost right away. She answered via email and said something along the lines of this: *Dear Claire, If your novel is half as funny as your query letter, you will definitely find someone. However, it won't be me.*

I couldn't believe it. Two whole agents weren't interested in representing me. What was their problem? And who needed a literary agent anyway? I'd just find my own publisher.

This probably sounds like a dinosaur story, but my first book was published in 2000, and back then you couldn't just Google "how to get published" or "how many agents should you query before you take matters into your own hands?" or even "how to find the right literary agent." I'd lost touch with my writer friends, mostly because I was embarrassed because they'd been writing all these years and I hadn't. I had no contacts, nobody to point me in the right direction, to buy me a clue.

The only resource I had was a great big book that comes out every year called *Writers' Market.* I flipped through a library copy, looking for a publisher that would accept unagented fiction submissions. I found one and submitted. The publisher asked for fifty pages, then the whole manuscript. And then they bought it.

The advance I received for that first novel was so tiny that I think I spent more on gas to drive to the handful of bookstores that would let me do book signings. I was okay with this. I was willing to work hard, to climb the publishing ladder rung by rung. I still had my teaching job to help pay our bills.

My book was well reviewed, and because of that, literary agents began to approach me. The problem was that I'd apparently signed away a second novel, not only unwritten but unimagined at the time, to that publisher for the same insanely low amount of money. I *must* have read the contract before I signed it, but I think I wanted to be published so desperately that I skimmed right over that part.

By this point I'd realized what a stupid thing I'd done. I'd written a new novel, and there was also a literary agent I really wanted to work with. So I hired a big New York publishing attorney to try to buy back the rights to my second novel. The publisher was willing to sell the rights back to me, but for five times what they'd agreed to pay me. And they wanted all the money up front, instead of when I sold the book "because they had no confidence that Ms. Cook would ever again attain publication." Ouch.

The publishing attorney wanted his fee right away, too, which turned out to be the exact same amount of money the publisher wanted. Double ouch.

I was a teacher at a little private school. My husband Jake was a land surveyor. We had two expensive kids, a sizeable mortgage, high property taxes. When I added up what I'd have to pay the publisher and the attorney, it was almost half my yearly salary. Before taxes. And, scariest of all, what if I spent all that money we didn't have, and it turned out the publisher was right and Ms. Cook never did attain publication again?

Sometimes you've just gotta believe in yourself. Jake and I took out an equity line of credit on our house. I paid the publisher. I paid the attorney.

My new literary agent sent the book out to all the big publishers I wouldn't have been able to get to on my own. There were overnight offers from two. Two more offers came in two days later. The book was set to go to auction. (I didn't even know a book could go to auction.) And then a two-book preemptive offer came in from one of New York's biggest publishers for sixteen times my annual salary as a teacher.

That book was *Must Love Dogs.*

PROJECT YOU

My daughter Garet and my sister Mary are both certified project managers. Their left brains are way more developed than mine, and they are plotters, not pantsers. When they speak about reinvention, it's in a language other than my own, and it includes otherworldly concepts like business model and business plan.

They're both really, really smart. Not that I don't think I can hold my own with the brighter crayons in the box, but it's a different kind of intelligence.

So, let's hear it from the project managers. Garet reminds me that while I'm a narrative learner—more comfortable learning from stories—other people might be more receptive to material synthesized into outline or bullet point form.

I've never really thought about it before, but it's definitely true that I'm a narrative learner. If someone tells me a story, I can often remember it in full detail years later. But when I read through a series of bullet points, by the time I reach the fourth bullet, I've not only forgotten the first one, but I'm kind of ready to shoot myself. I think about this for a while and then decide that since I have no aptitude for bullet points, if you need to come up with some as you read to connect the dots to your own learning style, then that's a great use for your notebook. And from this point forward, I will stop making cracks about bullet points.

"Lists," my sister Mary says. "I think I got into project management because I love making lists and crossing things off so much."

I try to imagine making lists and crossing things off as an activity that's satisfying, even fun, something that would give me a sense of accomplishment. Nope. I don't get it. Lists don't do a thing for me. But they might do something for you.

Here's how my sister Mary is approaching her own reinvention. While earning her B.S. in chemical engineering, Mary also juggled a work study job maintaining printers at the university computing center, where she learned to debug computer programs and eventually became a good computer programmer in her own right. The combination of the two sets of skills led her to a series of big jobs at big companies, from Xerox to Pfizer. When the "project management bug bit," she switched directions and went on to earn her M.S. in project management as well as several impressive certifications.

"Project management," Mary says, "is a great career for someone like me who loves structuring something, but then gets bored or sees a shiny object. Projects typically go one to two years, so there is always something new around the corner. Generally, once I get the teams and structure set up and chugging along, I completely lose interest."

Hmm, maybe we are related after all! I'd never thought of it that way, but writing a novel is its own kind of project management. You structure the world, shape every part of it, and then you let it go and move on to something new.

But back to Mary. More and more, she's been feeling the need to do something "that would let me apply my skills to do good in the world."

So Mary started making a list of global nonprofits. She eventually narrowed it down to one whose U.S. office is based in the state she lives in. "It was a crazy departure from anything I had ever done, but I was pretty passionate about their mission."

After thoroughly researching this nonprofit, Mary made a list of positives and negatives about the potential move, and another positive/negative list for her current far-less-than-perfect job with a big pharmaceutical company. When the right position opened up at the nonprofit, she did more research to see what type of skills they likely needed and to find out why the position was open, and she weighed her background against that.

"I decided there were enough positives to throw my hat into the ring, so I did." The nonprofit jumped quickly, and Mary spent a whirlwind two weeks in interviews with everyone from the CEO to the team she would manage. The next lists were her non-negotiables—vacation time, salary, benefits—which she shared with the recruiter.

Mary made it down to the final two candidates, and they went with the other one. "The experience gave me the confidence that I could find that match between my talents and my passions."

And now she gets to make more lists. "I'm doing the same thing with two other nonprofit companies right now. The more interesting one is a startup, risky but with high upward potential." I have no doubt that Mary will find a way to use her mega skills to do good in the world, and in the meantime she's enjoying the journey—and the lists!

NOT REINVENTING THE WHEEL

List-maker that I'm not, I still take the business end of things seriously. And while I think keeping in mind your unique life experiences, your special gifts, is really important when it comes to deciding *what* you want to do, when it comes to figuring out *how* you're going to build the scaffolding—the structure that supports your dream and keeps it from crumbling in the first strong wind—I'm not sure original is what you're going for.

My advice is to become a giant sponge and soak up everything people have already figured out about how to successfully navigate a journey like the one you're about to embark on. In short, while you'll certainly add your own embellishments, don't reinvent the wheel in this arena unless you have to.

If you're heading into Authorville, who is rocking a career like the one you want? Google her. Read her interviews. What's her story and how did she get there? Go to her website and use it as a jumping off point for your own design. Get on her e-newsletter list. What does she write about in her newsletters? How often does she send them out and what company does she use to send them? What kinds of things does she post on

Facebook? What does she tweet about? Does she use Pinterest? Instagram? What kind of physical events does she do?

Sign up for updates from cutting edge publishing sites like JaneFriedman.com, my personal favorite because I can always count on Jane to be both forward thinking and balanced, and ThePassiveVoice.com, as well as the more traditional Publishers Weekly and Shelf Awareness. Spend time at Writer's Café at Kboards.com and WriterUnboxed.com. Check out my writing page at ClaireCook.com. There's a ton of great information out there, and it's free.

If you want to be a travel blogger, Google "best travel blogs" and start following the ones you feel a connection to. Two travel bloggers with very different blogs attended the We Move Forward conference— Amy Angelilli of Adventure-Project.com and Julia Rosien of GoGirlfriend.com. Check out JourneyWoman.com, HoleintheDonut.com, WanderlustandLipstick.com, TravelingWineChick.com, and SoloTravelerBlog.com, too. Keep Googling to find the blogs that resonate for you and feel somehow connected to your vision for your blog-to-be—there are lots of great ones out there.

Thinking about opening a surf camp? A women's adventure camp? Google it up and start following the people who are already doing it.

If you want to open a wine bar for knitters, find out if anyone else has already done it. If not, research them both. What's the wine version of Writers' Café? Where do knitters connect and share?

I jot down these leads and resources in one of my notebooks. I bookmark the sites on my computer, too, but it's nice to know that when I can't find the bookmark, because it's lost in a million other bookmarks, or I simply forget that I've ever bookmarked it, flipping through my notebooks will uncover it again. I also write down anything these people have said or done that might possibly help me down the road, as well as their contact info in case I decide to reach out to them at a later date.

As for reaching out directly to these trailblazers, I encourage you to wait until you've done your initial research and have a specific question to ask. At least several times a month, sometimes a lot more often, I receive an email via my website along the lines of, *Hi Claire/Clair/Clare! I'm writing a book, too, and I'm wondering if I can pick your brain! I loved Must Love Dogs, especially the scene where (insert scene that was in the movie and not the book). Did you get to meet John Cusack/Dermot Mulroney/Christopher Plummer?*

I may well have sent emails asking perfect strangers to pick their brains, or worse, back before I knew any better. But now I know that it doesn't take much visibility in your field before the floodgates open and everybody wants to have coffee with you. Or they come up to you after an event where you've just expended huge amounts of energy sharing everything you can think of to help the entire group. Now they want to cut you away from the pack for some one-on-one time. As if there might be some magic trick you'll share only with them if they can just get you alone.

I've already shared it all, and if there's anything I've forgotten, you can find it at ClaireCook.com, where I share every helpful thing I can think of. I'm not holding back on you—I'm giving everything I've got, when I speak, on my website, in this book. Sharing what I've learned is a huge part of who I am and how I live my life.

But here's the truth: If I let everybody pick my brain, I wouldn't have a brain left. Time and solitude are the two things a writer needs and never has enough of. If I spent my days having coffee, I wouldn't be able to meet my own deadlines. And over the years I've learned that the phrase "pick your brain" not only sounds painful, but is often a tip-off that this person has no idea yet what she needs to know.

This doesn't mean you might not hit somebody at the right time—she might be in full procrastination mode and dying to have her brain picked. Also, my guess is that requests for one-on-one time might be less prevalent in other fields. So maybe if you're planning to open a drive-in theater or a bowling alley or a bakery, the people who are already doing it would love to have coffee with you.

But in the beginning, there are better ways to connect. If your paths cross in person, thank the person for giving a great talk/opening an inspirational restaurant. Offer some positive feedback—tell her what parts of the talk/elements of the restaurant resonated the most for you. Say you're looking forward to reading her work/visiting her restaurant again. Whether or not you connect in person, you can say these same things on Facebook or Twitter, or in a review.

Try to imagine how often that person is approached, physically or virtually, by people who are writing a book/opening a restaurant. Now double that number, maybe even triple it. So if you want to stand out from the pack, you're much more likely to be remembered fondly if you start from a place of appreciating this person's work. In my experience, very few people think to do this, yet when they do, I not only remember them, but I'm so grateful for their support that I genuinely want to help them down the road if I can.

Once I was explaining this to a group of writers in a workshop I was teaching. Everybody got really quiet. Finally one woman said, "You mean, I should approach the authors I love as a *reader* instead of as a writer? I never would have thought of that."

Try it. Support the people already in your field-to-be and build up some good energy with them. They'll remember you down the road.

When and if you do ask them for guidance, tread carefully. Have some specific questions ready and check their websites first to make sure they haven't already answered them there. Approach with grace and courtesy. Talk up their business/work to thank them for their kindness—it's the most memorable thing you can do.

NANCY DREW AND YOU

Just as remembering that thing you wanted to do before life got in the way can help you find your reinvention destination, revisiting something of special meaning to you back then can sometimes help you create a template of sorts to guide you on your journey.

Nancy Drew and I go way back: When my mother dies suddenly when I'm in fifth grade, I decide that spending time with Nancy is preferable to inhabiting my own life. So I disappear into my mother's worn blue copy of *The Mystery at Lilac Inn* and quickly work my way through the rest of her collection.

I like to close my eyes and pretend the pages smell like my mother, though they actually smell more like mildew. Even then I know you can always imagine something better than reality. Nancy's world is fair and predictable. Though she's lost her own mother, she seems to be doing just fine. She even has a boyfriend. And a snappy blue roadster.

I rediscover Nancy when I'm teaching writing to middle schoolers. I think you have to be an avid, joyful reader before you can be a writer, and some of the kids just aren't big readers yet. So we all lug in a crazy assortment of things—novels, magazines, comic books, manga, biographies, old encyclopedias. We swap everything around and curl up in corners all over the room and just read. I bring Nancy and, retro as she is, a couple of the kids really take to her.

I remember my own daughter's obsession with *The Babysitters Club*, my son's addiction to *Goosebumps*. My kids just couldn't get enough of them. They picked up reading speed. They eventually moved on to other books and became lifelong readers. The truth, as I come to see it, is that once you fall in love, really in love, with that first book, you'll never be able to stop. There will still be plenty of time to introduce the classics. I give Nancy full credit for that teaching epiphany.

I revisit Nancy a third time just before I begin writing my first novel in my minivan. I find my mother's collection on the dusty top shelf of our tallest bookcase. I curl up and read them all again, one after another after another.

I'm scared and Nancy is there for me. She teaches me not to write the boring parts, those long descriptive passages that Elmore Leonard famously called "the parts that people skip over." Nancy teaches me to keep my chapters short, and to end them in such a way that even if the reader tells herself that she's going to close the book and go to sleep after this chapter, she won't be able to.

Although our books are nothing alike, there are times as I'm writing my first novel and feeling my way into my own style when it feels like I might be channeling Nancy. That maybe I'll even get to drive her snappy blue roadster one day.

I still don't think you can be a writer unless you're a voracious and enthusiastic reader. Every book you read informs you in some way, helps you figure out what you'll write, and what you won't write, when it's your turn. As I continued to read and read and read, throughout my life and in a more targeted way with the Nancy Drew mysteries, a template of sorts for how to write my own novels formed in some mysterious place in my head.

I didn't do it on purpose, though in hindsight, choosing a model that hit major chords for me emotionally but was also a big hop and a leap away from what I was about to create, turned out to be helpful in a couple ways. It scratched that raw place where the best things come from and made it available to me. But also, since my model was far enough away from what I was trying to write, there was no chance that I'd lean on it too heavily and inadvertently imitate it, in substance or style, so I didn't have to worry about that.

I've used this template strategy since then as well. A few books in, I was really struggling to find the right ending for one of my novels. Nothing was working. The endings I tried just didn't feel right—they felt forced or fell flat. So without really planning to, I walked over to one of the bookshelves in my office and started pulling out novels randomly. I sat down on the floor, and trying not to even look at the titles or authors, I read the last two pages of each one. One after another, with barely a pause between them.

I remembered what a good ending felt like. And somewhere along the way, my own ending began to come to me. It was completely unrelated to the endings I'd just read, but they absolutely led me there.

So if you're an aspiring writer, think about taking a fresh look at a book that you once connected to emotionally but isn't too close to the one you're about to write. Use it as a loose template. *Ah, so this is what a good beginning feels like.* And then you write your own beginning. *Right, so this is how you introduce a character.* You can guide yourself through a whole draft this way, and it might make the journey feel a little less scary.

If I were designing a fancy portable restroom, I'd find the most elegant powder room I could, or remember the first truly decadent bathroom I ever stepped into, and use it for a jumping off point. I'd spend time on Pinterest, a great source for design inspiration.

If I were to open a restaurant, I'd head for one that always makes me feel hugged when I walk through the door. Even though they're not on the menu, it might bring back gossamer memories of my mother making homemade fish and chips for us every Friday—the real way, with the chips deep-fried and poured into a paper bag to degrease and stay warm while they waited for the haddock to cook. I'd take furtive photos of the restaurant interior with my phone and write down details—schoolhouse pendants, distressed interior shutters, candles in mason jars, a single edible nasturtium garnishing every dish—that speak to the vibe I want to create. I'd check out their website and their ads and their Facebook page.

Robbie Kaye is a classical/jazz-trained musician who has reinvented herself as a photographer. Whatever her medium, Robbie is a storyteller. Remembering her own mother and grandmother's weekly beauty parlor visits led her to her most well-known project, Beauty and Wisdom, a photographic essay of women in their 70s, 80s, and 90s at their weekly beauty parlor visits. It's truly the end of an era, and Robbie has traveled across the country to capture the last women to make this weekly pilgrimage to their local salon. Robbie's lens captures the real story, the story behind the story, that this tradition is not just about sitting under the dryer in curlers and being teased and sprayed within an inch of your life. It's about finding community and a sympathetic ear. Her photos are amazing.

Judi Powers was a powerful marketing executive. But she was looking for more: "After September 11th, I, like so many people, realized that life is too short not to live each day as fully as possible." But Judi had no idea what else she wanted to do to make a living. So she decided to try a variety of things, "from dancing (disaster!) to flower arranging (wonderful, but too depressing once the flowers wilted) to cooking (fabulous but fattening)."

Judi took her first jewelry-making class, and she was immediately hooked. She continued to take one class a semester or so for over ten years as she learned her craft and worked toward her reinvention. Perfectionism was the thing that nearly held Judi back from living her dream. "There is no perfection in reinvention. Period." When she felt ready to become a professional jewelry maker, she quit her publishing career and attended Fashion Institute of Technology's one-year jewelry design program. She considers herself a "recovering perfectionist" and is now the proud owner of Judi Powers Jewelry.

Judi makes sustainable, handcrafted fine jewelry and watches, and her work is incredible. Though it's stylistically very different from the jewelry she creates, the emotional template for Judi's reinvention was a monogrammed locket her grandmother gave her for her fifth birthday. It was the first piece of jewelry meant just for her, and the locket and the memories they triggered figured so prominently in her journey that Judi includes a photo and tells the story on her website.

Templates, emotional or more concrete, are one more thing to consider that might—or might not!—help you out as you take your own journey.

DO SOMETHING NICE
FOR SOMEONE

You're gazing through fog down that long windy road to your reinvention, which seems a gazillion miles away. It's easy to get needy when you're really struggling to figure out the next step and wondering how you're going to find the guts to take it. Believe me, I know.

But many of the best things that have happened to me on my own journey have been triggered not by me getting down on my knees and begging for help from every person I cross paths with, though I've certainly been tempted often enough, but by something nice I did.

"Karma is a boomerang" is one of the smartest things one of my characters has ever said. *Multiple Choice* is my novel about a mother and daughter who go to college at the same time and end up sharing an internship at a radio station. "Karma is a boomerang" is the sign-off for a crazy New Age radio show on the station called *Karyn's Karmic Korner.* It's also one of my favorite sayings.

That some kindness you put out into the world can boomerang back to you is something I believe with all my heart. This is not to say that I go around doing nice things all day long just to get something back. The truth is that sometimes it boomerangs and sometimes it doesn't. But still, whether it comes back to you or not, sprinkling kindness as you go is a great way to walk through the world.

So the next time you're feeling needy, consider doing something nice for someone else, who just might be feeling the same way. It'll give you both a boost and the other person will remember it. And it might even boomerang back to you someday in a big way.

The way the *Must Love Dogs* movie happened is one of my favorite karma is a boomerang stories: I'm on book tour for the *Must Love Dogs* paperback, and I've just finished an event at a charming independent bookstore in Vermont. Before I go on to my next stop, I sign extra copies of the book, which the events coordinator turns into a big tabletop display right as you walk in the door.

A day or so later, Gary David Goldberg, who created *Family Ties* and *Spin City* and *Brooklyn Bridge* and owns a house in the area, stops by the store looking for something to read. He picks up a copy of *Must Love Dogs* from the display. His five dogs are waiting for him in his car. He turns the book over and sees it's about a big Irish family. His wife, Diana Meehan, is from a big Irish family.

So Gary buys a copy. He later tells me that he drove straight home, poured a glass of wine, sat down in his favorite chair, and didn't get up again until he finished reading it. I've thanked my literary agent in the acknowledgments, so the next morning he calls her in NYC and asks if anyone has optioned it yet. And before my head stops spinning, an offer has been made and I've accepted it.

It's a cool story, and sometimes I stop here when I'm telling it, because it's such a happy ending. But the truth is that after a whole bunch of back and forth between agents and lawyers for both parties, all the details have been worked out and the final contract drawn up.

And then one day I get a phone call from my agent. I can't remember her exact words, probably because I go numb, but I can still feel her fury. She tells me Gary has withdrawn the offer, that this simply isn't done so late in the game, and that she can't believe she has to tell me that all this money is being taken out of my pocket.

I try to let it sink in, but not having a movie deal seems just as unreal as having one. So I reach for something positive. "Well," I say, "I guess the good news is Gary David Goldberg thinks I can write. Can you get me his address so I can send him a thank-you note?"

As I remember it, my agent sighs and says I am such a Pollyanna, and goes on, in her tough love way, to inform me that one does not send thank-you notes to people who pull out of deals. I persist. She emails me the address for Gary's company, Ubu Productions.

I begin my letter to Gary by saying I have no idea what really happened, and I realize I'll probably never know. What I'm hanging on to is how truly honored I am that he enjoyed my novel. I tell him I'm a huge fan of his work, that I'd first seen his name on the credits for *The Bob Newhart Show* when I was in college, and it got so I could pick out the episodes he'd written. And I go on to give him a detailed rundown of his own resume, like he doesn't already know it—all the great old shows, like *M*A*S*H* and *Lou Grant*, he's worked on. I end by thanking him again and wishing him well.

So that's it. I snail-mail the letter off to Ubu Productions in Los Angeles and go on with my life.

Maybe a week later, a fax (remember those?!) rolls into my office. Gary is in Vermont, where my letter has been faxed to him. He's just come back from a five-mile walk with his dogs to find it. He says that, in all his years in the business, it's the kindest, most humane letter he's ever received. He wants me to know that the reason he pulled out of the deal is that he's broken up with his agent, that Hollywood is an ugly business and he hates it and is never, ever going to work in that awful world again. And he didn't want to tie up my wonderful novel when it was at its most valuable.

I have to admit, as I read that, a part of me is thinking, *Oh, please, tie it up. I don't even care if you make the movie. Do you know how many bills that option money could pay?* But I know it's over and any groveling on my part won't be good for either of us. So I send him a short fax thanking him for explaining it to me, telling him how much I love Vermont, and wishing him lots of long walks with his dogs.

He faxes me back, thanking me for my fax and telling me a little bit about his dogs and his life in Vermont. So I fax him back, thanking him for thanking me and telling him a little bit about my dog and my life not in Vermont. We start faxing back and forth, his messages in his beautiful handwritten scrawl and mine sometimes typed and printed out, telling each other about our spouses and our kids, sharing crazy writer stories.

Two weeks or so into this, I get a fax from Gary that begins, "This is so much fun! It's like being pen pals but neither of us is in prison!"

And so my one and only fax friendship is born. I've often thought how easily I could have missed the whole thing. Gary doesn't do email, and I've only bought a fax machine because I thought I should buy *something* to make me look like a real writer when I got the first check for my first big book deal.

Gary's faxes are often hilarious, and trying to keep up with him helps my own comedic timing so much as we volley back and forth, the way playing tennis with someone who's better than you does. His faxes also become big family entertainment at my house. As soon as the fax machine starts chugging away in my office, my whole family comes running in to ask, "Is it from *Gary*?"

And then, maybe nine or ten months into this, my literary agent calls me again. "You are not going to believe this," she says. "Gary David Goldberg has put in another offer for *Must Love Dogs*." It's an even bigger offer than the first one, and this time the paperwork is signed on his end and ready to go.

I fax Gary to thank him and to find out what the hell is going on. He replies that he knows someone is going to make *Must Love Dogs* into a movie eventually, and when it happens, he won't be able to stand the thought of it not being him. And he wants me to know that if I hadn't sent him that first letter, he would never, ever have circled back to my novel. He would have optioned any other book in the entire world before he crossed paths with that agent of mine again.

The next day three beautiful lidded gift baskets, handmade from branches, are delivered to my house. The baskets are each a different size, with the largest on the bottom and the smallest on the top, creating a kind of steps-to-the-sky effect. They're filled with a decadent assortment of goodies. With them comes a note from Gary that says simply, "Here we go!"

That Gary and I are now friends makes all the difference in the world in the way the movie unfolds, at least for me, and I like to think for him, too. And just to add one more karmic twist, after my truly excellent *Must Love Dogs* movie adventure, I find out that Gary has always wanted to write a book. So the tables turn and I'm able to show my gratitude by mentoring him a bit—I encourage him, read his drafts, and reconnect him with my literary agent. She ends up representing him and selling the book, and quickly goes from being that agent of mine to "our Lisa."

Gary died in 2013. I'll miss my fax pal and his big heart forever.

MORE KARMA

Karma has boomeranged back to me on a regular basis, in ways big and small. Once I was asked to teach a writing workshop for a lifelong learning program affiliated with a prestigious university in another part of the country. Because of the way they were budgeted, they didn't have the money to pay for things like travel and accommodations for speakers, but they had a huge mailing list, a good-size advertising budget, and lots of media connections.

My publisher was flying me in to the area and putting me up in a hotel for book tour, so I suggested we link the two. I'd waive my teaching fee if they were willing to include a copy of my latest novel in the cost of the class, and also use the clout they had to help get the word out about my workshop as well as my new book.

Well, they rocked it. They got me appearances on network affiliates and interviews on local radio stations, put my workshop on the front page of their seasonal catalog and on the home page of their website, even featured it on a massive billboard on campus. They packed my workshop, and it was dream publicity for my new novel. The director of their entire program did me the honor of coming to hear me speak.

A little while later, someone from the *Today* show called this program director about something completely unrelated. In the course of their conversation, she happened to ask him if anything else was going on that *Today* should know about. He said they'd just had this novelist in to teach a workshop and she was one of the best speakers they'd ever had, that she'd written her first novel in her minivan when she was forty-five, and what had impressed him the most was how generous she was in trying to help others in their own reinventions.

He later said that I'd also stuck in his mind because I was the only instructor they'd ever had who'd been flexible enough to teach for free! (In my mind, I hadn't really taught for free. We'd made a fair exchange of what I needed for what they needed.)

And that's how I ended up being a *Today*'s *Woman*: The crew spends eight hours with me, at my house and at a hometown reinvention workshop I teach that night. I'm the type of person who can either look put-together or have a clean house, so I have to admit a lot of fake cleaning happens before *Today* shows up. It's all fun and games until they want some depth-of-field shots and start rearranging our furniture. As they move the couch, something I've never even considered as a possibility, I hold my breath and wait for a stray gummy bear from the '80's to roll out from under it.

The gummy bear never appears, but I learn, once again, that nothing worthwhile ever turns out to be completely smooth sailing. The *Today* visit is almost scheduled, then scheduled, then maybe not happening, then rescheduled. Finally, they're coming and soon. I call my landscape designer friend, Leslie Brigham, and ask if she could come over and make the window boxes and planters and entrances to our house look *Today*-worthy. Leslie is talented and super busy and it's the height of her season, but she's a great person, so she agrees to juggle. She shows up with a truckload of plants, a massive pile of mulch, and three strong workers, just as it starts to drizzle.

Jake and I roll up our sleeves and pitch in, too. The drizzle turns into a deluge. We're all absolutely drenched, but in a few hours the outside of our house looks great, and we don't even have to water.

About three days later, I wake up with the mother of all headaches. It feels like my brain has swollen and is too big to fit inside my head. It's not like anything I've ever experienced, and it hurts so much that I immediately think of my sister, Trish, who once survived meningitis.

I'm afraid to move, but I finally drag myself out of bed and walk carefully to the bathroom. There's no delicate way to say this, but when I go to sit on the toilet, I look down and my right hip and half of my abdomen are covered with a big, angry red bulls-eye.

Yep, Lyme disease. I call my primary care physician's office, blurt out my double emergency—rash/headache and impending *Today* visit. I'm not sure which half does it, but they tell me to come right in. I manage to brush my teeth and pull on a T-shirt and yoga pants. Jake helps me into the car and drives me across town.

My doctor takes one look and confirms that it's a medical textbook picture-worthy Lyme disease rash. The fact that my body has reacted so violently and suddenly means that I've most likely picked up the deer tick recently. Probably during our landscaping-in-the-rain stint a few days before. He says it's great we caught it early, and tells me he'll prescribe extra-strong antibiotics to make sure the Lyme is knocked out for good. The headache will start to go away as the antibiotics kick in. The antibiotics might make me nauseated, but I should take it easy and I'll be feeling better in a week or so.

Today is coming in three days. I can barely move. I'm sicker than I've ever been, and taking the antibiotics makes me feel even sicker. Almost everybody in my life tells me to get in touch with *Today* to reschedule. *They'll understand*, they all say.

But I know, I just know, that if I try to reschedule, the producers will cross me out on their whiteboard, fill in with another piece, and the whole thing will slip away. Mine is not a story *Today* needs to cover. It's not newsworthy and I'm not a celebrity. Karma may have boomeranged it to me, but my gut tells me that even karma can't get me a second slot. It's a one shot deal. Sick as I am, I have to buck up and do it anyway.

I don't know how I actually do it, other than that I just decide I have to, and so I dig down deep and find a way. My husband and son step up big time. My daughter flies in to help. My talented hair and makeup artist friend, Charlotte Phinney, comes to my house on the big day, tells me what to wear, camouflages the circles under my eyes, airbrushes me with many magic layers of makeup, and whips my hair into place.

I'm hurting, but once the *Today* crew arrives, adrenaline kicks in and I think I do a pretty good imitation of a healthy person.

Would I have done a better job if I'd been feeling perky? Maybe, but I still don't think that was the choice in front of me. It was take it or leave it. And if it's an incredible opportunity, and you're serious about your reinvention, I truly believe that if it's at all possible, you have to go for it.

Most of my karmic examples are not as dramatic as this, but they're pretty wonderful. My old friends and former students and their families still come to my book events and talk up my books, as do the people who've attended my writing and reinvention workshops or connected with me online. I get lots of email like this recent one: "Your generosity of spirit is refreshing and made me want to read your books, which I'm now burning through, one after another."

I am so grateful to these people for supporting my books and giving me the gift of my career. As one of my favorites Irish proverbs goes, "Always remember to forget the friends that proved untrue. But never forget to remember those that stuck by you."

Just something to think about as you wonder who is going to patronize your restaurant, stay at your bed and breakfast, rent your portable restrooms, download your music, and boomerang karma back into *your* life.

ON THE ISLA AGAIN

The speakers at We Move Forward are a veritable treasure trove of reinvention possibilities. After she was widowed at thirty-three, Angelina de Galdamez founded an orphanage in Guatemala, then turned it into a children's village to provide home, healthcare and education for 250 children. After that, she built Hotel Backpackers to provide sustainable funding and job training for them.

Kim Kraushar is the co-owner of Interlude Spas and a master instructor and trainer who presents internationally. She leads the team that teaches mindful movement classes at the conference and also a dance party that ends in a dip in the Caribbean ocean. You can tell how much she loves her work—she glows with health and happiness.

Katie Milton, Janeen's assistant, left her "cozy cubicle" at a large corporation in her mid-twenties. She has a blog called *We're All Here Because We're Not All There*, and she's on her way to becoming a life coach. She couldn't have chosen a more supportive audience to make her debut as a presenter.

Shelley Roberts is a business consultant who co-launched Women With Power, "a series of dinner and unique conversations between women from all walks of life to redefine what it means to have power as a woman today." She's sprightly and energetic and put together. She reminds us that light travels faster than sound and that people have an intuitive attraction or repulsion to us when they first see us. She tells us to think about "How do I show up when I walk into a room?" My hand reaches up to console my poor mid-reinvention hair. Oh, well.

Jerusha Akatzin, a representative of Consejo Maya Neuvo Sol (Mayan Council of Grandparents of New Sun) is at the conference to speak and perform a Mayan blessing. To be honest, when I scan the schedule I don't think I'll be all that into it. I wonder briefly if I can sneak off in the direction of the restroom and go do some more exploring on my own.

But I remind myself that I promised to be a full participant, and I stay. And I'm blown away. Jerusha comes to the stage with her mother and a younger woman, as well as a translator. Jerusha speaks lyrically and softly, and even though I don't understand them until they're translated, the rhythm of her words pulls me in. She punctuates her sentences by softly beating a handheld drum.

She tells us that we're all in this moment of rebirth underneath the sun. "We know what it's like to be thirsty . . . And sometimes happy. It is an injustice not to listen to our own soul. Spirituality is not passive . . . .."

She's hypnotic. The audience is spellbound. "As we stand in the womb of this circular room," she continues, "the theme of today is weaving our dreams. In each of us there are many women . . .. If you feel the feeling to push the limits, push them. You are not going to die."

She taps the drum with the heel of her hand and stays silent until the sound fades away. "We're all the same. We all have the same heart. And we all bleed every moon."

Jerusha taps the drum again and says something else in her Mayan dialect.

"We must listen to the voice of our grandfather," the translator says.

"Grandmother," Jerusha corrects in English.

The entire room breaks into laughter, including Jerusha and the translator. And in this moment I realize that Jerusha could probably do her whole speech in English. But she's giving us the gift of her ancestral heritage. The musicality of her language. The kind of otherworldly ceremonial wonder I used to feel as a kid in Catholic school when the Mass was still said in Latin and I couldn't understand a word those priests were saying.

Jerusha has found yet another way to be authentically herself, even as she dedicates her life to preserving a culture that has been marginalized and is in danger of disappearing.

Almost one hundred women follow her out of the building. We form an enormous circle on the expansive lawn overlooking the ocean so Jerusha can "play the drum in the womb for each one of you."

Jerusha and her mother walk around the circle. They stop in front of each woman. Jerusha's mother sprinkles water from a flower on her, then Jerusha looks her in the eyes and holds her gaze as she sings some kind of prayer and plays her drum. She's got the kind of intense blue-gray eyes that evangelists and saints and fortunetellers and sometimes crazy people have. They seem to bore right through you and into your soul.

When it's my turn, I feel it. The beat of the drum in the room of my womb. The connection to Jerusha and her power and her past and her song and her eyes and her spirit to my spirit and where I've been and where I'm going. A tear surprises me as it rolls down my cheek, and I thank her.

When she moves on to the next woman, I wipe my cheek and put my sunglasses back on. I look past the women across from me in the circle and see that the younger woman with Jerusha has stepped away a re-spectful distance to take a cellphone call under the shade of a palm tree. She's laughing and flipping her hair and gesturing with one hand.

Instead of making the moment feel less magical, the cellphone incident makes it feel more so. As if our journeys aren't really that different after all. As if whatever our lives and aspirations are, we're all in this together. We really are all the same.

THE BEST PART
OF YOUR ENERGY

My trick to juggling it all is deceptively simple. I wake up early and finish my daily pages before I let the rest of the world in. I stumble out of my bedroom, pour a cup of coffee, grab a handful of nuts, and sit down at my computer.

I'm not quite awake yet, and I haven't had time to start procrastinating, to start thinking about all the things besides writing I should be doing. I'm at my most creative before I'm fully awake, maybe because it feels like I'm closer to my last dream than I am to my first load of laundry.

I drift into writer world without fighting it too much. I get into my zone or find that place of flow or whatever it is, that headspace where capturing the words is still hard but also completely compelling and somehow natural. On my best days, I pretty much stay there until my pages are done. On more difficult days, I float in and out, but I persevere. On my worst days, I do it anyway.

When my pages are finished, I take a long walk or hop on the elliptical machine, then I move on to interview questions, my website, email, Facebook, Twitter, Pinterest. They're all important, but the most important thing is always the book I'm writing, because without that my whole house of cards would collapse.

For me, the virtual kiss of death is to start my day by checking email or doing social networking. It's so easy to get sucked in, and before I know it hours have passed and I've put my best energy and creativity into trying to compose the perfect tweet. Even a quick peek is invasive, because suddenly I'm thinking about how I'm going to answer that email later in the day instead of focusing on the pages in front of me.

If I still had young children who needed diaper changes and breakfast, obviously this system would not work so well. I know lots of women who get their kids on the school bus and then dig into their work. Or they put the kids to bed and use the quiet hours of the night to do the work that will move them forward. One lucky woman I know, who has four young children, checks into an inexpensive hotel one weekend a month while her husband does kid patrol. She says she finishes a month's worth of work in two marathon days and nights.

I know other women who escape the distractions of the world around them by holing up at the library or the nearest Starbucks. This wouldn't work for me because I'd spend all my time people watching and eavesdropping. It might be a carryover from my swim mom days when I learned to dive into the solitude of my minivan to write, but what works best for me is to disappear into an empty space behind closed doors. I've written entire novels in the corner of mid-renovation rooms filled with boxes.

I'm fortunate enough to have an office with a big window now. But I keep the blinds closed while I work, because otherwise I'd be gardening in my mind, wondering if some of those Lenten roses should be moved around the corner, or if we need another ornamental grass right *there* and what is the name of the kind with stripes and I wonder if the garden center has any. Maybe I should take a quick ride over there and find out.

I'm amazed when people rent beach houses to inspire them as they work. I wouldn't get a thing done. Assuming a beach house was an option, I'd rather work at home in my cave of an office and save it as a reward for finishing a project.

I think the important thing is that you identify the freshest part of your day that's available and stake your claim on it. Use every minute of it for the thing that's going to propel you toward your destination, whatever it may be. Lock the time in if you can so that it becomes a habit. Protect yourself from distractions and intrusions in a way that works for your life and your personality.

Tie it into your system for accountability, whether it's my dorky calendar or a portable kitchen timer or cellphone alarm that you set for the length of a work session. Or if you need it, use an app like Freedom to shut down your Internet access for a set amount of time. There are lots of them out there—just Google it.

Reinventing your life is a marathon, not a sprint. I believe that the people who are successful at realizing their dreams are putting the time in, not just once in a while, but consistently, day in and day out. "Diligence is the mother of good luck," a proverb dating back to the 16th century says. I think *we're* the mothers of our own good luck. Diligence—along with tenacity, determination, and guts—is the fuel that gets us there.

Which means that finding the right thing is key. Factoring in short breaks between books and a few days off for good behavior here and there, I've essentially been writing seven days a week for over a decade. Short of sleeping and eating and reading and laughing, I can't think of another thing in the world I could make myself do seven days a week.

ISLA TIME

On Isla Mujeres, one moment I'm on island time and real time slips away. It's old Mexico, where you can walk the cobbled streets instead of having to stay behind the walls of a gated resort. Things happen when they happen, and when they take even longer, everyone shrugs and says, *It's Mexico.* The next moment, everything speeds up and I can feel time *whooshing* by, propelled by the sea breeze, and I want to lunge for it and make it slow down.

I start asking the women attending We Move Forward if they have any good reinvention stories for me. I want to capture as many as I can before I go back home.

I chat with Julie Fraga, the official conference photographer. Julie began her career as a theater actress and later became an assistant director, mainly episodic television and made-for-TV movies, as well as the occasional feature film.

And then Julie went on vacation with a friend to Isla Mujeres. On their last night, they had dinner at a restaurant, and she fell head over heels for the man who owned it. Julie went back to LA, but Isla and the restaurant owner kept calling out to her. So she extricated herself from an on again/off again relationship with an actor and went back. She's been married to her restaurant owner for twenty-three years. "Would I have moved to Isla if I hadn't fallen in love? Probably not." But Julie has reinvented herself as a website and app developer as well as a photographer. She's also a partner in a new production company, Lucky Cat Pictures. "If you wake up most mornings feeling happy and excited about what you're doing, perfect!"

Julie goes back to taking conference photos, and I wander off to collect some more stories. A woman comes up to me when I'm standing alone. I've met her already and I love her big, welcoming smile and quick laugh. Now she leans in close and whispers, "Do not use my name. Say only that I am a woman from Brazil."

"Got it," I say.

"I have many big issues for many years, caused by very serious things. But I spend hours and hours in good therapy, and because of that I finally find love when I am forty. And I am married."

"Great," I say, "good for you. So your reinvention story is that, after many years of struggle, you found love and now you're happy?"

"Well," she says, "my in-laws are awful. Horrible." She lowers her voice. "Remember, do not use my name. Say only that I am a woman from Brazil. But my step-grandchildren are wonderful. I am a child again through them. We play and play together, and they are the joy of my life."

"That's so great," I say.

"And my boss. For many years I work for a powerful woman who treats me terribly. Nothing I do pleases her. No amount of work is enough. And then one day I find the courage to tell her what I think, that she can never treat me this way again."

"Good for you. And then you quit?"

"No. But everything between us changes. And now I can continue to work for her."

We hug and I thank her for sharing her stories. I find myself turning them over and over in my head as I try to process them. In the end I think they remind me, as a writer and as a person, how different our lives are, and how every tweak, large and small, ordinary or exotic, can have an extraordinary impact when it's your life.

At ten months, Liza breaks the record for the youngest We Move Forward participant when she refuses to be left behind in the hotel with her doting entourage, which consists of her father and grand-mother and her two older brothers. I make a beeline for her and scoop her up and walk her around to give her mother a break. Mom Danyelle is an attorney with her own practice. She was narrowly defeated in a district court run, and plans for another one are underway. She calls Liza her "oops child" and appears to be thorough-ly enjoying her own oops reinvention. I think how cool it would be if Liza looks back one day and finds inspiration in the fact that she made her women's conference debut at such an early age.

Brigit is at the other end of the conference age spec-trum. In her late 70s, she's smart and funny, more vibrant and alive than many women half her age. Her independence and joie de vivre make her an amazing role model for all of us, and everybody adores her.

One morning I catch up with her as she walks across the long bridge to the resort and our big circular meeting room. I thought I'd heard every *Must Love Dogs*-generated question there could be by now, but Brigit asks me if dogs go through menopause. I laugh it off, but she approaches me later in the conference to tell me that she was serious, that she really wants to know. Okay, I just looked it up. No, they don't. As an unspayed female dog ages, her twice yearly cycles might become irregular, but she's still fertile. So now we both know, Brigit.

On the final night of the conference, Brigit sips a glass of red wine and tells a group of us how much she's hoping to stay alive for another year so she can make it to the next conference.

My bet is that she'll not only be alive, but thriving.

THE STARS AND YOU

Back in my swim mom days, before I retired to my minivan to write, I learned a lot watching all those swimmers. Born-with-it talent is a rare and beautiful thing. The innately gifted swimmers sparkle brighter than the others. When they swim, their bodies might have a physical buoyancy that makes them ride higher in the water than their teammates do. They could be shy and awkward on land, but they move naturally and joyfully in the water like little dolphins, as if it's their true habitat. Their movements are graceful, poetry in motion, but incredibly efficient, too. The first time they race as an eight-and-under, they might even break the pool record.

These kids are the stars. It's unmistakable. Everybody can see the brilliant future they have in front of them. Their parents might invest in a private coach, or a series of private coaches. The dad starts to follow the colleges with the best swim teams, even though their swimmer is barely in elementary school. The mom does a search to find out which country will host the summer Olympics in eight years, maybe even downloads a Fodor's Guide to the area, just for fun.

And then one day a few years later, that clunky girl, the one with the weird backstroke who swings one arm funny, blows right by this little star and wins the race. Everybody thinks it's a fluke, but the clunky girl wins again. And again. In the freestyle, and then in the breaststroke. And finally her weird backstroke takes her all the way to league championships.

While the stars have been coasting along on their star power, the kids who've had to work so much harder because they weren't born with that innate ability, have been doing just that. Lap by lap, week after week, year after year, they've conquered the things that didn't come easily to them. And at some point, they nip at the stars' heels, and eventually they pass them by. Passion and hard work trump talent. In the end, whoever wants it more wins.

Burned out stars are everywhere. You meet them at a cookout or online, and they're quick to tell you their story. Their writing was so genius that one of the best MFA programs in the country gave them a full ride. Before the ink on the diploma was even dry, they had an offer from a big time publisher. But the editor actually wanted them to make some changes to the manuscript before she'd plunk down any money, and these stars were certainly not going to change word one unless they were paid for it, and maybe not even then, their work was so amazing.

"How long ago was that?" you ask.

Twenty years. Or thirty. Or fifty.

In the original book of the *Must Love Dogs* series, Sarah has a date with a guy like this. As they exchange stories over coffee, Ray describes himself as your basic underachiever, but he's quick to add that he had a lot of potential once. He waits for Sarah to prompt him, then goes on to say that he was a hockey player in high school. He was good, really good. Everyone was sure he'd play professionally. Senior year he had some offers from colleges, but they weren't big enough. So his parents thought that if he went to prep school for a year, he'd get bigger and better and the top colleges would come knocking. So he went to prep school. And it didn't happen. All these years later, he wears his almost-stardom like a badge, and he's still not over the injustice of it.

"It's so not fair," we say when these things happen to us. And we're right. Life isn't fair, and I'm not sure how the rumor got out there that it was. Life can be ridiculously tough. And when it is, we have two choices: give up or be tougher.

Meanwhile, while the stars are being stars, the non-stars keep working toward their dream, whatever it is. They put the time in on their craft and set their egos aside so they can get better, across feast and famine, over obstacle after obstacle, and through lots and lots of rejection. In the end, they get where they're going.

If you were born with talent, good for you. But if being a star hasn't gotten you where you want to go yet, or even if it did for a while and now you've dead-ended, you might want to forget you have it and roll up your sleeves and get to work.

What got me to my first published novel was not that I won a contest to name the Fizzies whale in the three-and-under-category four decades before. Or that two decades later I spent a year as a visiting student at Harvard and studied with Robert S. Fitzgerald, who translated *The Iliad* and *The Odyssey*, or even that he gave me an A. (Though clearly I still remember it!)

Sure, I had some talent. But it didn't get me where I needed to go. What got me there was finally acknowledging I wanted it, shaking off the fear, setting a goal, breaking it into manageable chunks, and making myself accountable until I'd completed the novel. And then doing it over and over again until I had a career.

Achieving a dream takes passion and hard work and tenacity. You can't buy those qualities anywhere. Nobody else can give them to you. Not a teacher. Not a mentor. Not a career or a life coach. They can help and encourage you, if you're lucky enough to find the right one. But the buck stops with you.

As Nora Ephron said, "Above all, be the heroine of your life, not the victim." So whether you're a natural born star or not, let it go. Especially the poor me part. If only this or that had happened or hadn't happened. If only I were more talented, luckier, smarter, wealthier, better looking, younger. Shake it off. Banish those thoughts from your mind.

If you're willing to put in the work, you're enough.

THE FEAR FACTOR

When asked what's standing in their way, right behind money and time for my Facebook research team is fear. *Fear. Fear of not being able to support my family. Fear. Fear of failure. Fear. Fear of success. My fear is standing in my way. I'd like to not be afraid of taking chances. My own fear of success and failure. Fear. Fear. Fear.*

As I write this book, I feel fear sometimes, too. What if I'm not sharing the right stories, the right tips? The things that will inspire you to finally dig up your buried dream or figure out what you want to be when you grow up. The sparks that you'll be able to fan into flames. The tools for not getting lost or running out of gas along the way. What if this book isn't what I dreamed it could be? What if I let you down?

Or, after pouring my heart and soul into eleven novels, what if this book is The One. The book everybody loves so much that they tell their family and friends and all the other dreamers and seekers they cross paths with that they just *have* to read it? Will that kind of success make the rest of my books feel like failures?

Knock it off. All of us.

Fear is a fact of a well-lived life. If you're not afraid, you're still in your comfort zone, miles and miles away from your reinvention destination. If your game plan is to put your car into Park and let your engine idle until you're not afraid to hit the road again, you might as well make a U-turn right now and head back home where you're safe and sound.

As Anaïs Nin said, "Life shrinks or expands in proportion to one's courage."

"Of course you're afraid," a character in my novel *Time Flies* says. "We're all afraid. There are only two choices: afraid and boring."

FEAR OF SUCCESS

Let's start with fear of success. Success is certainly better than the alternative, but it can be terrifying. How will you handle that first interview? That grand opening? What will you *wear*?

My *Must Love Dogs* movie experience was both amazing and absolutely petrifying. Talk about out of your comfort zone.

Fear reared its head right away: Gary David Goldberg wants to meet me. He and his wife are going to be in Boston, and he wants to take me out to lunch at The Four Seasons. I resist the urge to wiggle out of it, or to ask him if we can change the location to somewhere a little less intimidating, like maybe Dunkin' Donuts. I manage to exchange my writing sweatpants for something more lunch worthy. I transport myself from the 'burbs to the big city via my trusty minivan.

It's not until I find myself standing on the edge of Boston Public Gardens, across the street from The Four Seasons, that I remember. Almost two decades before, an old friend of Jake's and mine, who was working as a painter—house, not fine arts—stepped on a nail at a construction site. It went right through his work boot. He didn't have health insurance, so he just pulled it out and went back to work. Several weeks later, his blood poisoning turned into gangrene and he ended up in the hospital, still with no health insurance and now in danger of losing his leg.

His friends rented a hall and threw a party to raise money for his medical bills. Everybody donated raffle items. One of the old friends, Billy Dowd, had a job casting extras for *Spenser: For Hire*, the television show starring Robert Urich, which was being shot in Boston. Billy donated a chance to be an extra for a day on the show.

I won it. And because Billy is a nice guy, he doubled the prize and said Jake could be an extra, too. Our firstborn was two, and we'd been juggling our schedules so that one of us was almost always with her. But my friend Dayle kindly offered to watch her, so we spent a crazy long day walking back and forth and back and forth some more for an episode of *Spenser: For Hire*.

Some of the scenes that long ago day had been shot in the exact section of the Public Gardens I'm standing in now. The other scenes were shot across the street—inside the very same hotel where I'm about to have lunch with Gary David Goldberg almost twenty years later. How bizarre.

Back then the extras were herded like cattle into a holding room off the lobby. We had to whisper, and if we ate anything, we were supposed to be careful we didn't leave a mess. We were only allowed to use one bathroom, and we had to ask permission first.

This time around I'm pretty sure I can use any bathroom I want.

I cross the street and stand in front of the entrance to The Four Seasons. When I was an extra, I wasn't nervous at all (although, completely off-topic, I do remember wondering if there was any significance to the fact that, as the director kept coupling and re-coupling the extras for walk-throughs, not once did he put my real life husband and me together). I had nothing riding on it, no acting aspirations, no dreams pinned to my success or failure, so it was all fun.

But now, I'm terrified. What if I say something stupid and Gary hates me so he lets my option run out while he turns his attention to a book written by another author who never says stupid things and makes that book into a movie instead?

Two doormen are standing in front of The Four Seasons. "Can I help you, ma'am?" one of them asks.

"Omigod," I say. And then I blurt out the whole story. How I wrote this book and Gary David Goldberg wants to make it into a movie and now I have to have lunch with him and how I'm scared to death to go inside.

"Listen," the second doorman says. "The guy is lucky to get your book. You're in the drivah's seat."

"You got this," the first one says. "You just march right in there like you own the friggin' place and knock him dead. We'll be right here if you need us."

My new best friends the doormen hold the doors open for me. And sitting on a sofa directly across from the entrance, where he's just witnessed every bit of my frantic exchange with the doormen, is Gary David Goldberg.

He shakes his head. "Workin' the crowd on the way in, huh?"

I think I might have dropped a fork, or maybe it was only a napkin, but other that that, we have an awesome, ridiculously long lunch. We talk and talk for hours—about our families and books and politics and sports and how we're going to work together without ruining our friendship. About our visions for the movie. Which scenes from the book do I think need to be in the movie? Which actors do I picture? What music? We later joke in interviews that I made five thousand suggestions and he took exactly one, and neither of us could remember which one it was.

Actors sign on. Warner Bros. greenlights the movie. My life keeps getting more exciting—and with each step the fear level ramps up, too. My family and I are flown out for the table read, the first time the cast meets as a group and reads the script together, which is often held around a kitchen table at the studio. Gary being his magnanimous self, this table read begins with a catered dinner by the pool at his Brentwood mansion.

Adorable California girls with pink scarves tied around their necks park the cars. Heat lamps warm the already perfect early evening air. Gary whisks me around, introducing me to the actors.

Christopher Plummer kisses my hand and then steps back. With grand Shakespeare-worthy elocution, he announces, "The author is here."

"Cut it out," I say. "You're Christopher Plummer."

"Hey," he says. "I haven't had a good gig like this in a while."

While we're chatting, Diane Lane puts her hand on my sleeve and tells me she likes the top I'm wearing. "Mar*shalls*," I say, and she cracks up. She knows I'd been a teacher before I became an author, so we talk about her daughter's school and the PTO and ideas for birthday parties.

As I'm standing with my daughter Garet, John Cusack walks up to us. I've already chatted with him, so he reaches his hand out to Garet and says, "Hi, we haven't met yet. I'm John."

Dermot Mulroney, who I've also already chatted with, walks over. "Hi," he says, holding out his hand to Garet. "I'm Dermot."

"Hi," my daughter says. "I'm, I'm, I'm . . .."

My cooler-than-cool, about-to-turn-twenty-one daughter has completely forgotten her own name.

Finally, she points to me. "And that's my, uh, my, uh—"

"*Mother?*" I say.

My son's high school English teacher has promised him an A if he gets John Cusack's autograph for her. Kaden fights his own fear and manages to get it, though I don't remember if the A ever came through.

When everybody adjourns to the massive library for the table read, the fear factor escalates again. We gather around a humongous wooden table with the actors. Gary's wonderful assistant, Heather Green, has thoughtfully provided personalized copies of the script not just for me, but for Jake and our kids.

Jake and I look more closely at our scripts. Printed under our names are character names. Characters who have lines we are actually supposed to read. Now. In front of all these actors. And my sweet, shy, land surveyor husband has to read a date scene with Diane Lane.

Jake goes pale. He gives me his *get me out of this* look. I give him my *Sorry, but I am so totally in over my own head that you are on your own* look.

And somehow we both get through it and every fun and scary thing that comes after it.

So, yes, success can be mind-numbingly scary. When it happens, you'll figure it out. You'll dig down deep and take a lesson from that old Nike ad and Just Do It. But if you don't keep chugging along, if you let the fear of success stop you in your tracks, you'll never have the star problem of handling it.

If my shy husband, who has had a public speaking phobia since third grade, can read a date scene with Diane Lane in front of a room full of actors in a Brentwood mansion, you can do anything.

As my friends the doormen said, "You got this."

FEAR OF FAILURE

So moving on to fear of failure. If what you're doing is significant, of course you're going to fail. In fact, if you can't remember the last time you failed at anything, you might want to step it up a little. You might be playing it way too safe and easy.

After successfully climbing a more traditional ladder, Sarah has recently reinvented herself as sales and marketing director for a Swedish startup. "Give yourself permission to fail," she says. "And fail and fail. Failing is fantastic—the more you do it the better you are for it and the less you notice it. This sounds so cliché, but it really works!"

Failure can be painful, or embarrassing, or gut wrenching, and sometimes all of the above. I fail on a regular basis, so I know. What works for me is to give myself about twenty-four hours to be borderline suicidal about it, to wallow, to whine, to cry my eyes out. To obsess. To rant. To second-guess myself as well as pretty much every move I've made since kindergarten.

And then I shut myself off. I roll up my sleeves and get back to work. As C.S. Lewis said, "Getting over a painful experience is much like crossing monkey bars. You have to let go at some point in order to move forward."

An old writer friend of mine once lost about six months of her life over a bad *New York Times* review for one of her books. She just couldn't let it go. She went from friend to friend, railing about the unfairness, the persecution, the humiliation. When she ran out of friends, she started at the beginning and went through them all again. And again. And again.

From where I sat, it wasn't a great review, but it wasn't that bad. And, hello, her book was reviewed in the *New York Times*, where the vast majority of writers will never see their books reviewed. And there were definitely quote-worthy phrases in her review that could be pulled out and slapped on the paperback edition, as well as a few sentences that, even though they weren't necessarily intended to be positive, I thought made the book sound interesting enough to entice people to read it.

But the worst thing was that the whole time she was bemoaning one bad review, she wasn't writing. Giving failure that much power is, in my humble opinion, just plain ridiculous. And I think it can ultimately become one more way to procrastinate.

It's often the *anticipation* of failure that creates the fear, which can stir up even more self-destructive behavior than actually failing does. You shut down, because if you don't finish the work, you won't have to find out whether you failed or not.

Or, in one of my own self-destructive quirks, I find myself not opening certain emails or listening to certain phone messages because I'm afraid to hear something I don't want to hear. It's such self-defeating avoidance, and it ratchets up bucket loads of anxiety. I know this and yet sometimes I do it anyway.

Again, when it happens, I let myself be pathetic for about a day or so, and then I force myself to look or listen. Even when there's bad news waiting for me, it's also a huge relief to just get it over with so that I can wallow in it for awhile and then shake it off and move on.

I think it's a good idea to put a failure system in place. I love the Japanese proverb, "Fall down seven times, stand up eight." So simple, so streamlined. I admit that in my own failure system I've embellished this slightly by including whining, but it's still relatively efficient that way and it works.

Essentially, you've got to tie your failures into tenacity. One of the most-quoted passages from my novel *Seven Year Switch*, which is always popping up somewhere online, is this: "If Plan A doesn't work, the alphabet has 25 more letters. (204 if you're in Japan!)" Sometimes it can feel as if we've failed our way through most of the alphabet, but if the dream is important enough to us, eventually we'll either find a plan that gets us there or fine-tune our dream until it works for us.

At times there's no rhyme or reason to failure. It just sucks, and all you can do is move on. And maybe even turn the failure into high octane "I'll show them" fuel to propel you forward.

But often failure comes with a lesson, and if you can put your ego aside enough to tap into it and allow it to teach you something, failure can be a huge gift.

I know how hard it can be to hear these things, but they are golden nuggets. Your new wine café for knitters is profiled in the local paper, and it's not good. But the negatives are spot on and so eminently fixable, if only you can hear them. What if you made the changes and then thanked the journalist for her valuable insights and invited her back?

Your manuscript is rejected by an editor, but she takes the time to write a note saying she found the story compelling, but the dialog felt forced and the characters weren't quite believable. That editor has just bought you a clue! She's told you how to turn this failure into a success. Sure, you might find another editor who thinks the manuscript is fine as is, but tweaking the dialog and sharpening the characters will only make your book better, which is the ultimate goal.

I think it's really important to learn to get out of our own way so that we can take this information in. If you're anything like me, your initial reaction is to get defensive, because if the other person is crazy, or a hack, then it's not really a failure. There are entire TV shows built on this premise: restaurant is failing, restaurant owner is in total denial, kick-butt star rides in on white horse and gets right in restaurant owner's face and tells him his food stinks, his menu stinks, his décor stinks, his management skills stink. Restaurant owner fights it. Star keeps pushing. Restaurant owner sees the light. Restaurant is completely revamped and saved. Kick-butt star rides off to next episode.

So fail and fail again. The more you fail, the more you'll grow. Every failure is an opportunity to figure out how to do it better the next time, a chance to bounce back instead of crumbling into dust. If failure comes with a lesson, take it. If it doesn't, put it behind you and move on. And when the fear of failure rushes in, push past it and try to see it as a sign that you're getting closer to your destination.

Because if you're reinventing your life, it's good to be afraid, even very afraid. That's how you get to all the best places.

THE DOG STICK

As I walk the streets of Isla Mujeres, Katrina and the Waves are singing "Walking on Sunshine" in my head. I pick up my pace to match their quick tempo, waiting for the endorphins to kick in after a morning of mostly sitting.

I love to walk, and as a writer, it's one of the best tools in my bag of tricks. I think it's the repetitive rhythm that does it—maybe it lulls the resistance and self-doubt to sleep so ideas can float to the surface.

Walking helps me figure out what I'm thinking, what I want to write next, how I can fix what I've just written. Most of all, it makes me feel better. As Noreen says in *The Wildwater Walking Club*, "It's not about the vanity. It's about the sanity. Walking always helps."

I cross a stretch of beach, sunglasses and my funky sun hat shading me from the hot sun, my sneakers sinking into the soft white sand as I weave in and out of the tourists on lounge chairs and the servers bringing them their margaritas.

Then I work my way out to the street and stop under the shade of a bougainvillea-draped arbor for a long sip of bottled water. As soon as I set off again, a guy whips around the corner on a scooter and almost takes me out on the narrow, cobblestone street. Even that doesn't break my bliss.

The only thing bothering me is that I can't stop looking at all the animals.

I've been trying not to see them since I got here, but they're everywhere. As the sun sets, they congregate on the street around the corner from my hotel, bathed in coolish shadows. Short-haired street dogs and cats stand around, as if they've found their marks on a movie set and the garbage that's been left by the curb is just a prop, and not something they're waiting for the cover of darkness to dig into to keep them alive for another night.

I try not to look into their eyes. But there's this one tuxedo cat I can't look away from. Its black and white formality seems all wrong for life on the street. Last night I stopped and we watched each other for a while.

"I wish I could take you home with me, honey," I whispered. "But I can't."

It blinked its sea green eyes at me and nodded, as if it knew this before I did.

This morning the tuxedo cat and some of the others are still there, looking tired, like they've had a rough night. The dogs and cats are well fed on restaurant scraps, but still I want to take them all home with me, give them overpriced pet food and silly toys and fancy beds to sleep on. I fill a stray takeout cup from my water bottle and leave it in front of the tuxedo cat before I head off for my own breakfast.

Now, as I turn around to walk back to the conference, I try not to notice the animals asleep under trees
and in shady entryways. A little girl sits on the sidewalk playing with tiny chicks in a cardboard box. I'm
pretty sure the next We Move Forward speaker is going to make it even harder to look away.

But I make myself go hear her anyway. In her first
life, Alison Sawyer Current was a successful potter.
When she and her husband Jeff, who's the conference
sound man, moved to Isla Mujeres, they built an artsy
waterfront home with an indoor pool surrounded by
two mosaic walkways. It had a great big pottery studio.

And then, as Alison says, she "got hit with the dog
stick." So she turned her life, and Jeff's, upside down to
create Isla Animals, a non-profit organization that
sponsors spay and neuter clinics, vaccinations, and
animal care.

Alison tells us that all a dog wants is a human being
of its own. When it doesn't have one, the dog gets
hopeless and loses its spirit. Complicating matters on
Isla Mujeres is that it's "not part of the Mexican culture
to treat dogs with respect. If something happens to
one, you just get another. So we start with outreach to
the children and teach them how to honor their pets.
And if they don't, look out for me, because I will scoop
them up and take them away." She laughs, but she
clearly means business. My guess is there's not a person
on the island who would mess with her.

"Short-haired street dogs can survive on the street,"
Alison says. "Spaying and neutering them means fewer
dogs and therefore more food to go around." She tells

us that veterinarians volunteer their time, and her beautiful pottery studio has been turned into the spaying and neutering room.

"But breed dogs need our help," Alison continues. "Why would you adopt a dog from here when there are plenty of homeless dogs closer to home? The best answer I have is that there's no one in Mexico to take them. We'll place them anywhere there's a good home—frigid temperatures, snow, whatever. They don't care about weather. All they care about is getting a human."

A group of us take a field trip, walking along the beach to Alison's home, which locals call La Casa de los Perros (The Doghouse). I tell myself over and over again that I will not fall in love with a dog. I will not adopt a dog. No matter what.

"Most rescues hate getting puppies," she tells us, "because they die. My puppies don't die." That she has the power to keep puppies alive is something you don't even question. Alison radiates the courage of her convictions, fueled by an endless stream of passion. It's no surprise that all the other shelters in the area send her their puppies.

As Alison unlocks the tall gate to the wall surrounding her house, we hear them. The gate swings open and there are puppies everywhere—skittering around the driveway, jumping up against the chain-link enclosure of a long run. Alison frees the dogs in the run. We *ooh* and *ahh* and pet them, and they wag their tails deliriously and jump and lap our faces. Field trippers and canines troop together into the house.

We scale the mosaic ramps, circling on either side of the indoor pool. The pool has been drained in the interests of dog safety and sits there empty, like a dream from another lifetime. The dogs who come in with us mingle with the indoor crew. There are maybe two dozen in all, though Alison tells us she's sheltered as many as forty-eight at once.

Dogs run around everywhere, nails scraping cool marble tiles. Most appear to be young, puppyish if not quite puppies. A massive stainless feeder is well-stocked with dry food—it might be tough out there on the streets, but there is no food insecurity at La Casa de los Perros.

"Come see the babies," Alison says. I know better, but I follow her up the stairs along with the other women anyway. In the center of a makeshift playpen are four of the cutest fluffy brown puppies I've ever seen.

Alison starts scooping them up and handing them out.

I take a step back. "Aww," I say. "What kind of a mix do you think they are? And how old are they?"

"I have no idea," she says. "Somebody put them in a cardboard box and then threw the box in a trash can and closed the lid."

When she hands me one of the puppies, I'm a goner. Those eyes, that puppy smell. His name is Mighty Mike and he wiggles his way up and buries his head in the crook of my neck. He digs his nails into the loose weave of the brand new cotton top I'm wearing. And even when he rips a little hole in it, trying to claim me as his new home, I still think he's adorable.

I bounce him like a baby for a while, and then one of the other women reaches out for a turn to hold him. I try to hand him over, but Mighty Mike is not having any part of it. He simply won't let go. He wiggles up higher, manages to squish more of himself into the crook of my neck. He's chosen me, and he's not taking no for an answer.

"Uh-oh," one of the women says.

"Must love dogs," another woman says.

CHECKING IN

So, where are you? Have you picked your reinvention destination, figured out your version of my two pages a day, and found a way to make yourself accountable? Have you chosen a notebook? Are you using it to jot down anything and everything you come across that might possibly come in handy down the road?

If so, good for you. Just keep putting one foot in front of the other until you find your rhythm, and your reinvention starts to take on a life of its own. And remember, as my heroine in *The Wildwater Walking Club* says, "Even big changes happen one step at a time."

If not, let's try to figure out why. Is it shiny object syndrome? Analysis paralysis? Commitment phobia? Maybe you should take a long, long walk, or go to sleep with your notebook under your pillow. When you get back, or wake up, make your best guess. Lock it in and get to work. Remember, even though you have to give it your all for it to be successful, this doesn't have to be your only reinvention. Life is long, if we're lucky, and there will be plenty of time for other reinventions farther down the road. But if you don't pick one and get moving on it, you'll never get to any of them.

Are you starting to choke? It could be that you're trying to figure out the entire route to your destination, which you can't possibly know at this point. In the beginning, try to look at it as more of an exploratory journey.

Even twelve books in, if I start to think about the whole book, the whole loooong slog ahead of me, instead of just putting one foot in front of the other and writing today's pages, it totally freaks me out. It's too much, too overwhelming, especially in the beginning before I've got a bunch of pages behind me. How will I possibly live through so many words and make it all the way to The End?

And yet I do, again and again, in large part because I've learned to transcend my big picture doubts so that I can tunnel in on what needs to happen today.

E.L. Doctorow said, "Writing is like driving at night in the fog. You can only see as far as your headlights, but you can make the whole trip that way." I think that's a great way to look at any reinvention journey.

Okay, what else could be causing you to stall out? Is perfectionism rearing its ugly head? I know what a challenge perfectionism can present. You have this perfect, beautiful image in your head, and when you try to get it down on paper, or with whatever medium you're using, the results just don't measure up. You're devastated. You're embarrassed that this pathetic attempt is your best shot. Maybe you can't do this thing after all. Maybe you don't even want to.

That kind of perfectionism is deadly, and it can absolutely poison your dream. So don't allow yourself to judge your early efforts. Just keep going. As you improve your focus and your aim, you'll get better. You have to give yourself permission to really stink at this thing you want to do until you figure it out. If you nitpick yourself every step of the way, you'll never get far enough down the road to be able to find out what you're capable of doing.

As a novelist, the thing that works for me is that I have to suspend my disbelief as I write my first draft. I try not to think too much and I just stay open and feel my way through. I imagine I'm a sculptor and I have to get that big messy slab of clay on the table, and once it's all there, I can tweak and prod and shape it into anything I want it to be. But I'll never get to the tweaking part if I don't get that scruffy draft on the page first.

Are you trying to get through this reinvention thing by locking your jaw and grinding your teeth? Lighten up. Loosen up. Once I was hanging out with my landscape designer friend Leslie while she was working. She held her arms wide to stand in for the branches of one of the trees she was about to plant. Her body became the tree trunk, and as she jumped from planting spot to planting spot, she scuffed the location for each tree with the heel of her work boot. When she finished, she'd created a swoopy half-circle of trees-to-be. "There are no straight lines in nature," she said. "Only sexy curves."

I think of this often as I try to find the sexy curve from one scene I'm writing to the next, instead of gritting my teeth and barreling straight at it like a freight train.

Whatever your destination, play with it a little bit, try to find the sexy curve. Unclench your jaw and have some fun. Because even if what you're choosing to do is really, really hard, the point is to make your life better, not worse.

LITTLE CAT FEET

If I were writing this as a novel, Mighty Mike would be on that plane home with me. I'd be sneaking him out of the carrier jammed under the seat in front of me so I could hold him. A *rebozo*—a traditional Mexican shawl—would be draped over one of my shoulders to camouflage him.

Or I'd endure a sad flight home alone, followed by a sleepless night, followed by an epiphany, and then I'd fly back to rescue both Mighty Mike and Tuxedo Cat.

I can still see them both. I've even dreamed of them.

Pamela Kramer would have found a way. She's an elementary school reading specialist. Because of her love of reading, and to ensure that every spare surface in her house would be perpetually overflowing with books, she became a national book reviewer without giving up her day job. As if that's not enough to keep her busy, she also fosters dogs. And lots of them.

The apple doesn't fall far from the tree, as they say, so when Pam's daughter and son-in-law, Abbie and Clark Kopelman, were living in China, they rescued two puppies and a dog. One puppy died, but the other puppy and the dog lived. Pam went to China and brought them to the States. She's fostering Chloe, the dog, and seeing her through the surgeries she needs as the result of being hit by a car as a puppy. Rollo, the surviving puppy, was adopted by an older couple who adore him, and he spends every afternoon with their adopted Chinese granddaughters.

Years before, when Pam and her family were visiting her mother in Florida, her kids found two stray dogs outside. So, of course, Pam invited them in. The family checked everywhere they could check, but no one had reported them missing, and because the area shelters were overrun with animals, Pam didn't want to leave them behind. It was too late to get vet certificates so they could fly home with them. Pam's mother happened to have a new car being delivered to her from the city where Pam lived. When the drivers arrived with the car, Pam managed to talk them into letting the dogs ride back with them, a trip of over one thousand miles. Pam's brother met the truck, kept the dogs overnight, and Pam and her family picked them up the next day. They found homes for both dogs.

There are so many wonderful ways to make a difference, just as there are so many worthy reinventions, but you can't choose them all. Sometimes you've got to just say no.

Especially if you've just said yes.

We adopted our dog Daisy Mei, a shar-pei/Lab cross that later inspired the puppies in the original *Must Love Dogs* novel, from a shelter. Her mother was a purebred shar-pei who escaped one day and ended up pregnant. Because the likely fathers were not purebred shar-peis, the owner washed his hands of the mother-to-be and dropped her off at the shelter, where she gave birth to eight puppies.

The puppies looked like wrinkled black Labs, almost like raisins. When they pulled themselves up to a standing position against their chain-link nursery, all that loose skin fell down and covered their butts like wrinkly tutus. They were so adorable, a long waiting list to adopt them formed. Our son begged. Our daughter begged. They tag-teamed us. We got on the list.

One of my former students happened to be volunteering at the shelter. When he saw my name on the list, he told the director, "If I were a puppy, that's who I'd want to live with." And thanks to him, at eight weeks Daisy was ours.

She was a bit of a drama queen—awful with other dogs, but good with people, especially when they were giving her lots of attention, and gentle with small children. We couldn't have loved her more. She had a great life, and gave us a better one.

When we moved from Massachusetts to Georgia, she was getting up there. We piled blankets and her bed on top of all the stuff crammed in our Element, and she rode high up on top of it as if it were a throne. She spent her first two nights ever in hotel rooms. She loved it all—hotel strangers telling her how sweet she was, riding up and down on the elevators.

We made it to the suburbs of Atlanta. She loved our new house, the contemporary windows with their pano-ramic views of squirrels, the lack of steep Victorian stairs. We walked and walked and walked with her, miles every day, and she couldn't get enough of all these new sniffs.

And then one day: Daisy walks a few hundred yards and can't go any farther. Just like that. She's almost fifteen, and it turns out she has congestive heart failure. So for the next six months, we love her up.

We buy an expandable ramp. She prances right up it, her pointy tail wagging, thrilled to have easy access to the car. We drive all the way to the park. She walks down the ramp, makes a small circle around the parking lot, and then she walks back up the ramp and we drive all the way home. It's the ritual she still wants, and we keep it going for her as long as we can.

After that's beyond her, we drive her around so she can bark at the dogs we pass, something we've been trying to get her to stop doing her whole life. "Way to go, Daisy," we cheer as she barks her hoarse bark.

When she stops eating, she spends most of her time on blankets on the floor of my office, keeping me company while I write and try not to cry. Jake is often on the floor beside her, or out in the kitchen trying to come up with something, anything she might eat. After a lifetime without people food, eggs work for a day. Bacon for half a day. At night, she moves to her bed in our bedroom, and we pet her and pet her, and she thanks us with little snorty sighs.

On a bathroom break in the middle of the night, she goes into convulsions in our driveway. We know it's time, and the look in her eyes says she does, too. The next night Dr. Katie Billmaier, a wonderful vet from

Lap of Love, comes to our house and helps us give her a beautiful, dignified death.

Later that night Jake says, "I can't do this again. Ever."

As the days and months go by, we talk and talk about it and finally agree. We've been taking care of kids and/or pets for almost the entire time we've been together. We've loved them all, but it's time for us now. We'll travel, have some fun. We'll be footloose and fancy-free, just like when we were first dating.

We find a rental that looks like a tree house on a deer-filled marsh with distant views of dolphins playing in the ocean. It's at the tip of Hilton Head, with miles and miles of gorgeous bike trails and beaches that go on forever. We bike and walk, walk and bike. Watch the deer and dolphins play.

And when we get home, a feral cat has given birth to four kittens under our front porch.

YOUR LIFEBOAT

Once you've logged enough solo miles that your reinvention destination starts to take shape, it might be time to let a few people in on your road trip. For me, that point usually comes when I've finished writing the first draft of a book. For other kinds of journeys, it might come earlier.

After all the road trip imagery, I know we're mixing metaphors here, but one of the best names I've heard for this kind of support group is *lifeboat*. Who do you want to ride out those gale force winds and churning seas with you? Because if you're reinventing your life, sooner or later you're going to run into some stormy weather.

At this point, and probably at every point to come, it's important to make sure letting other people in is not a stall tactic. For example: *While so and so is reading my first fifty pages, I don't have to write my two pages a day, because what would be the point of actually writing while I'm waiting for what could be crucial feedback that might change the whole book.*

Or: *I really don't feel like working today, so I think I'll use that block of time to meet so-and-so for a glass of wine. I'll tell her everything, and we can brainstorm!*

When it's time, choose these people with care. Personally, I'd rule out the know-it-alls and the glass half-empty people. It's important to navigate this reinvention yourself and not turn your power over to a know-it-all, which is really seductive at this stage. Because when you're scared, who doesn't want someone to take you by the hand and tell you what to do? But know-it-alls tend not to know anymore than we do—they just think they do. As for the glass half-empty people, I'd rule them out simply because I don't need that kind of negativity pulling me down.

But on the other end of the spectrum, I also don't need the people who love *everything*, the ones who will tell me that leopard print miniskirt I just bought looks fabulous. And then actually let me walk out the door wearing it.

We all need constructive honesty, often one of the hardest things to come by, and we need it presented in a clear, kindhearted way that cheers us on rather than tearing us down. If you can find a handful of people in the world who can and want to do this for you, you're incredibly fortunate. And because karma is, in fact, a boomerang, you'll also want to do it for them. There's your lifeboat.

I've also come to believe that you can divide the entire world into givers and takers. I do really well with another giver, because we both simply decide we'll do whatever we can to support each other. We can each ask for what we need, even if it's pathetic or embarrassing, and as soon as we do, we're already looking for ways to reciprocate.

But when I get mixed up with takers, it doesn't go well. I start off by pretending they're givers, because I want them to be. I do something nice, and because they're takers, they ask for the next thing. So I do it. And they ask for something else. It doesn't feel right, but I think there must be something inherently wrong with me that I would notice their lack of reciprocity, that I'm the kind of person who *keeps score.*

So I tell myself I should practice being more Zen about letting go of outcomes and learn to give simply for the sake of giving. By about the fourth or fifth ask, I find myself biting my tongue so that I don't offer any more help. And then I decide I don't want to be the kind of person who intentionally withholds support, and so I start planning my exit strategy. *What a user,* I think as I walk away, but the signs were there all along, and I could have saved myself a lot of unnecessary aggravation if only I'd read them.

But when you find the right person, it's just the best. A rising tide lifts all boats, as the old proverb goes, and supporting each other not only helps both of you get where you're going, but also makes the experience more fun.

Groups can be a bit more complicated. To borrow from that old Henry Wadsworth Longfellow poem, when they are good, they are very good indeed, but when they are bad, they are horrid. And the confusing thing is that groups can start off really well, and then when you least expect it, they turn. I've come to think that, while some groups can stay fresh for decades, others simply have a shelf life. So enjoy them while they work for you, but if you start to notice a slight stench, know (or at least hope!) it's not you and get out.

You can start your own reinvention group from scratch. Ask around to see if anyone knows anyone who's embarking on a new journey. Put it out to your Facebook friends. Your group could meet on a regular basis via Skype or Google Hangout or in a private Facebook group, or simply email one another.

You can search around for existing groups, online as well as locally. Maybe you can find a strategy group. Or a women in transition group. Or a small business or entrepreneur or artist or writing group via Meetup.com. Even if the group you find doesn't have the right click, you might be able to connect with a couple of like-minded souls there. And then you can spin off another group with them that does work for you.

Or take a course or workshop—maybe running a small business, designing a website, building your platform, or something more specific to your particular reinvention. Classroom settings are a great place to connect with people who might fit into your lifeboat.

When I teach reinvention and writing workshops, we often do a group activity I call speed networking. I make everybody stand up, walk around the room if it's possible, pivot around at their chairs if it's not, and find a person they haven't spoken to yet. When everyone is partnered off, I tell them they have to ask each other three questions: Where are you? Where are you going? What can we do to help each other?

There's always moaning and groaning, and I get that. It's hard to talk to strangers, let alone reveal yourself to them by giving what is essentially an elevator pitch. As Erma Bombeck said, "It takes a lot of courage to show your dreams to someone else."

But I insist, and so they do it. I give them a few minutes. And then I yell "Switch!" and they have to do it again. And then a third time. By this last pairing, the room absolutely buzzes with camaraderie. Emails are exchanged. Friendships are sparked. Lunch or dinner plans are made. Lifeboats sometimes even start filling up.

When I try to bring the activity to a close, people simply won't shut up, which on the one hand makes me so, so happy, but I also have lots more to cover before we're out of time. So I have to dig up my old teacher's voice to get them back in their seats.

At almost every single workshop where we've done speed networking, a handful of people approach to ask me to be their partner. I always redirect them back to the group. These people might have come to this workshop because they think I have all their answers, or because they want to connect with me, or even to see if I'll jump in their lifeboat.

But the truth is that what they really need is to connect with the other participants in the workshop. The ones who are on the same stretch of their reinvention journey, maybe a mile or two ahead of or behind them on the road. These are the people who have the time and the inclination to exchange progress emails or do a weekly Skype chat with you. They can proofread the brochure for your bed and breakfast while you critique their wine café for knitters website.

I can't. In a perfect world I'd love to, and sometimes I miss the days when I might have had the time. But I've been on the road a little longer, and I can barely keep up with my own To Do list now, so my sharing and support has to take other forms now, like this book. But if you're trying to start a group, feel free to post about it on my Facebook author page or tag me in a Tweet, and I'd be happy to help you get the word out.

So take to those open seas! And start filling that lifeboat. As William G.T. Shedd said, "A ship is safe in harbor, but that's not what ships are for."

And as Mark Twain said, "Twenty years from now you will be more disappointed by the things that you didn't do than by the ones you did do. So throw off the bowlines. Sail away from the safe harbor. Catch the trade winds in your sails. Explore. Dream. Discover."

One thing to remember though: As important as it is to build a supportive network, don't become so focused on hanging out with all these interesting new people in your life that you start to lose sight of your own destination.

LISTENING

I'm walking the streets of Isla Mujeres again. Journey is serenading me with an imaginary rendition of "Don't Stop Believing." As I listen, a part of me wants to sing along with them at the top of my lungs, but it's early so I resist.

Hidalgo Street is just waking up. The pockets of shade are still cool. A shopkeeper has finished cleaning inside and now dumps a bucket of water on the cobblestones just outside. She sweeps it around with a broom to clean the street in front of her shop, a long-handled dustpan tucked under one arm. As on any island, water is at a premium here, and I imagine that same bucket of water washing her dishes before it made its way downstairs to the store and then out to the cobblestones.

While I walk, I think about how hard it is to decide who you're going to listen to. I know that should be *whom*, but it sounds way too pretentious to my ears that way. And besides, our language isn't set in stone—it's fluid and ever changing. Just the way ginormous and wackadoodle have, for better or worse, found their way into mainstream dictionaries, I think it's only a matter of time before whom gets left behind in a pompous cloud of dust.

Do I listen to the waitress at the breakfast place who just told me I'd love their homemade rosemary bread, even though this is the first time we've laid eyes on each other? How does she know I like rosemary, or even bread? Do I listen to the boomer couple I just passed on the street because they smiled and said good morning and seemed somehow familiar, as if we might have gone to high school together? They could turn out to be ginormous wackadoodles.

With each book I've written and each decision I've made during that same stretch of time, more and more I've learned to listen to that voice inside of me that knows so much more than I used to give it credit for knowing. As you learn and grow, in some ways you become your own expert. Nobody else gets what you're trying to do the way you do.

But there are also times when I'm way too close to what I'm writing, and I can't tell anymore. It could be the best thing I've ever written, or the worst, and at that point I have absolutely no idea which one it is. I'm simply not capable of making the call. And even beyond that, the right input can add layers and dimensions to my work, things that I never would have thought of in a million years.

In the beginning, I invited way too much feedback. When you do that, lots of the feedback you receive can make sense in different ways, but when you put it all together it can feel completely contradictory. And suddenly your work has turned into a big hot mess and you're standing there holding your head trying to figure out how you're going to live through this.

But first of all, I think it's a good idea to step back and make sure you really *want* honest feedback. I have spent chunks of time thinking about other people's plans or work and then offering them the most helpful advice I could come up with. It wasn't until afterward that I realized all they really wanted me to do was tell them how brilliant it was. I would have loved to, but the truth was it wasn't there yet. And they weren't ready to hear that, which means they probably shouldn't have asked me, or anyone else, for advice in the first place.

When I'm ready to hear it, I've found some ways to help me get the most out of the feedback I need. If I'm working with an editor, I honestly try to take every single comment to heart. Because even if her suggestion feels totally off base to me, the fact that she didn't get what I was trying to do means that I haven't pulled it off yet. And if she feels that way, there will likely be other readers who do, too, which again means I've got more work to do. So if I think A and she suggests B, I try my hardest to find a C that works for both of us. Sometimes I can't, sometimes A is the only way, and in that case I'll push to hang onto it. But almost always there's something I can tweak to make the book better for both of us.

I'll also reach out to a small group of people who are kind enough to read for me. One might have specific knowledge of the field my heroine works in or a place she travels to or might have gone through a similar experience, such as a divorce or a corporate buyout. One might be a huge reader who has also read all my books. One might be another writer who has strengths where I have weaknesses, or is just really good at isolating the things that need more work. One is always my husband Jake, because he's so detail-oriented that he always finds small discrepancies and typos that everybody else misses.

Even though I'm looking for different things from each of these people, I'm also looking for consensus. If everybody flags the same paragraph and tells me they got a little bit confused here, or had to read this sentence two or three times, then I have some fixing to do. If everybody really likes that one snippet I wasn't so sure about, then yay, it works! If one person says something that doesn't resonate for me, and no one else chimes in with the same thing, I might make a small tweak to keep us both happy, or I might ignore it, whichever feels right.

In other fields, you could connect with a variety of people individually to present your version of my rough draft and ask them to give you their feedback. Or you could invite a group of them to get together with you, either in person or virtually, as part of a focus group.

Posting a question on my Facebook author page can give me immediate feedback or input, its own kind of group expertise. There's wonderful diversity in the people who see the post, ranging from loyal readers and previous workshop participants to old friends to people who just randomly ended up on my page. I'm really grateful to have this cross-section of opinions at my fingertips, and I never underestimate this collective Facebook wisdom.

I think it's important to remember that there are many kinds of expertise. No single person has all the answers you need. Also, our world is changing at such lightning speed that it's never been truer that, as screenwriter William Goldman once said about the film world, "Nobody knows anything."

So the guidance you're looking for will most likely come from a series of conversations. Rather than trying to hunt down a single guru, you'll most often be better served by pulling in knowledge and wisdom from a variety of carefully chosen sources to help you with your very specific situation.

And then you run all that input through your own filter and boil it down to what you need.

TIMING

Timing, if not quite everything, is at least something to consider. In a nutshell, I think you have to be ready to jump when an opportunity appears. Once again, *Must Love Dogs* has been one of my biggest teachers.

The Hollywood premiere of the *Must Love Dogs* movie is held at the mammoth Cinerama Dome on Sunset Boulevard. Months before, I was fortunate enough to get to hang out and watch the filming of the preschool scenes on location in San Pedro. I also sat in my very own director's chair with my name on it, autographed by all the actors to surprise me, as I watched the interior scenes being shot on one of the Warner Bros. sound stages. Sandra Bullock was shooting a movie in the soundstage just across from *Must Love Dogs*, and once when her movie wrapped early for the day, she sent her movie's barbeque over to our movie. I felt like I'd escaped from a studio tour bus, and any moment security was going to catch me and escort me out.

Now I'm thrilled that the fact that my name is on the movie poster entitles me to four tickets to the premiere, which means my husband and kids and I can all go. We're even given a suite at the Hollywood Roosevelt, down the hall from Diane Lane and Josh Brolin's suite. I'm grateful for every moment, every single experience. It's like being a contestant on that old game show *Queen for a Day*, except that I don't win a refrigerator.

I have no expectations for the premiere, other than thinking it will be fun and we'll probably get free popcorn. I wander Hollywood Boulevard early that afternoon with my daughter, poking around in all the tourist shops. I buy a knock-off Gucci bag shaped like a dog and a pink feather boa collar to clip around its neck, and decide it's only fitting to carry a copy of the book to the premiere in it. Clearly I'm thinking like a tourist rather than an author whose movie adaptation is about to premiere in a few hours, since I also buy a refrigerator magnet with a picture of the Hollywood sign on it.

By this point I've heard premiere stories from other authors. The one that sticks in my head is from an author whose name must not have been on the movie poster because he only got two tickets to his premiere. He brought his mother. The day came and they pulled up to the red carpet. The limo driver rolled down the window and gave his passenger's name and said he was the author.

As the driver got out to open the doors for the author and his mother, the event publicist leaned into her microphone. She announced his name and told the long line of media people standing behind the ropes on the edge of the red carpet that he was the author.

"Nah, we don't want him," a television reporter standing with his cameraman said loudly. Everybody else in the long line concurred with a headshake or a brush of their hand, or just ignored the announcement entirely. The author and his mother slunk along the length of the red carpet as quickly as they could and disappeared into the theater.

I've warned my family what to expect and I'm not really worried about it. I mostly want to watch the movie. Gary has shared every draft of the script, as well as a few short promo clips, but he hasn't wanted me to watch the whole thing until tonight.

It's early on a hot summer night, and the sun is still relentless. Our stretch limo pulls up. The driver lowers his window, gives my name and says I'm the author. He opens our doors and the event person announces me. I get ready to be ignored.

Well, it turns out that not only have the actors not arrived yet, but unbeknownst to me, one of the Boston affiliates has asked *Access Hollywood*, which airs on the same network, to get some footage of me so they can show it on the local news that night.

"We want her!" the crew from *Access Hollywood* yells.

And because *Access Hollywood* wants me, *Entertainment Tonight* yells, "We want her!"

And then *Xtra* wants me. And then everybody in the whole media line wants me. The event publicist starts escorting me toward the line. "How do you feel about director Gary David Goldberg changing Mother Teresa, the St. Bernard in the book, to a Newfoundland in the movie?" a reporter yells.

"I would have been fine with a possum," I yell back.

And so I walk along the red carpet, which is actually a dog-themed green faux-grass carpet dotted with fire hydrants, taking questions from the media line. After I finish chatting with the big outlets, the event person pulls me aside and whispers that I've done the important ones, so I can stop now if I want to.

"Are you kidding me?" I say. I talk to every single one of them, including the guy from a radio station in, I think, Singapore at the very end of the line. I do thirty-five interviews on that green carpet. The paparazzi are even yelling "Claire, Claire" and taking my picture when I look. At one point I ask a group of them if they are really the paparazzi because they seem so much nicer in person than I've heard they are.

And the next morning I awake to find out there is a picture of me, holding up my knock-off dog purse with a copy of *Must Love Dogs* peeking out, on the front page of *The Hollywood Reporter*. And in an AP piece that is picked up by hundreds and hundreds of publications, Michael Cidoni writes that in his twenty-five years of covering Hollywood premieres, he has never seen an author have as much fun at a premiere as Claire Cook. And of course, "*Must Love Dogs* author Claire Cook says she would have been fine with a possum!" is just about everywhere.

This was the year I turned fifty, which in Hollywood years I'm pretty sure is at least eighty-two. My green carpet media blitz was a total long shot, and I was not in any way prepared for it or expecting it to happen. A minute or two later one of the actors could have arrived and the media would have dropped me in a Hollywood minute. But in this tiny window was a colossal opportunity to get the word out about my books, and when that happens, you've just got to go for it.

Eventually my long-suffering family and I make it inside the theater. And I'm right—not only do we get free popcorn but also free soda, both delivered to us by handsome tuxedo-clad waiters. We're even seated in the front row of the first balcony, with the actors surrounding us.

Way down below in front of the movie screen, Gary stands up to speak.

"None of us would be here tonight," he begins, "without Claire Cook and her wonderful novel. I started out as a fan of her work, and we quickly became close personal friends, and I now consider her one of the few people in the world I can always count on for the truth presented in the kindest way possible."

Behind me, some of the actors hoot. Dermot Mulroney catches my eye and gives me a thumbs-up. I'm stunned. I'm overwhelmed. It's one of the most beautiful moments of my life.

Anything can happen. It is never, *ever* too late.

TIMING TOO

Okay, so fast-forward a few years with me. I write another novel. My editor jumps to a different publisher and I follow her. I write another novel. And maybe even another. Somewhere around this time I start to notice that whenever I'm in a bookstore, large or small, I no longer see more than the occasional copy of *Must Love Dogs* on the shelf. It's been published in four editions—hardcover, trade (big) paperback, mass market (small paperback) and movie edition (also a trade paperback.) And I'm used to seeing at least a couple of those editions, sometimes even all of them, at just about every bookstore I venture into.

Around this time, whenever I'm on book tour, booksellers around the country start telling me how disappointed they are that they weren't able to get their hands on any copies of *Must Love Dogs*. Because another publisher is sending me on tour, as in paying for it, and because in traditional publishing the emphasis is always on the newly published book as opposed to your body of work, at first I just apologize to the booksellers and shrug it off. My job is to go out there and talk up my new book.

And then one night, after a successful bookstore event for my latest release, a bookseller says to me, "Do you have any idea how many copies of *Must Love Dogs* we could have sold tonight?"

I have always felt that if a reader enjoys one of my novels, she'll want to read all the rest, so it doesn't really matter which book she jumps in on. So to have the book that everybody wants, which will eventually lead them to my other books if they like it, suddenly become unavailable just doesn't make sense.

When I get home I start calling bookstores randomly to see if they have any copies in stock. There are a few available here and there, but that's it. So I send an email to my literary agent detailing the whole thing. My agent sends a notice to my former publisher reminding them that they are contractually bound to keep this book in print and available to bookstores and giving them a certain number of months to do just that. The publisher says of course we will, thanks so much for reminding us, or something to that effect.

The time period runs out. I do another book event. Yet another bookseller tells me how disappointed she is that she was unable to order copies of the book all her customers want a signed copy of. I ask some bookseller friends to try to order it. I email my agent, who checks into it from her end. The publisher has not gone back to print.

My agent sends a legal notice to the publisher saying that because the contract has been breached, the rights of both *Must Love Dogs* and the other novel of mine they own, *Multiple Choice*, should revert to me immediately. The publisher signs off on it.

And just like that I own two of my novels again. I can't believe it happened, that the publisher didn't think *Must Love Dogs* was valuable enough to go back to press for even a small print run. Maybe it's because I've moved on to a new publisher, so they're over me. Another factor might be that traditional publishing tends to overlook their backlist books because they're so focused on the books about to come out.

Whatever the reason, I now own my most valuable book to date. Ebooks haven't begun to take off yet, so I don't even know quite what I'm going to do with it. But every instinct I have tells me that someday I'll be really glad I have it.

MORE ON TIMING

My point in sharing these two very different stories about timing is to encourage you to stay alert for moments of opportunity, no matter how unexpected. When they happen, jump on them. As Carl Jung said, "Synchronicity is an ever present reality for those who have eyes to see."

Even though my particular examples might be miles away from your own reinvention, other kinds of opportunities will absolutely come your way if you keep your eyes and ears open. You're thinking about starting a travel blog and one of the travel bloggers you're following announces that she's about to hang up her luggage tags and shut down her blog. Email her and start a conversation—maybe you can take over her blog rather than starting from square one.

Deb Witte took a leave of absence from teaching and started taking classes toward a graduate degree as a media specialist. She walked into a coffeehouse to do some homework and ended up talking to the owner for two hours. The owner was ready to move on and offered her a lease agreement to take over the coffee-house.

Deb had twenty-four hours to make her decision so she could drop her course load by the cut-off date to avoid paying a huge penalty. Was this simply shiny object syndrome, or was it a better fit? Sometimes you've just got to make your best guess.

Deb jumped. "Three coffeehouses and three retail design shops later, my friends joke that I am a serial entrepreneur, as I have been fortunate enough to sell all my previous businesses to someone who walked through the door and said they'd like to buy them."

DeAnn saw a press release for a new company and really liked what she read. "So I wrote a blind email to the info address just saying so, and telling them to keep up the great work. I am now working for them!"

When she turned forty, Debbie found herself not only going through a volatile divorce, but she was diagnosed with a brain tumor. "Life couldn't be worse. I was worried about what would happen to my children if I died on the operating table." Before her surgery, while she was doing her banking one day, she heard a car honking at her. It turned out to be her old boy-friend, the first love of her life at eighteen. They exchanged stories. Just like that he stepped back into her life, taking care of Debbie and her children through an eighteen-hour surgery and months of recovery. They've been a family for thirteen years now and have a beautiful son together.

When Leslie was laid off from her corporate job, a childhood friend who was a children's book editor asked her to write children's stories for them on a contract basis because she'd always enjoyed her Christmas letters.

Years ago, Sylvia was planning to babysit for the son of her pastor and his wife while they traveled to Mexico on a mission trip. Two weeks before the trip, the wife discovered she was pregnant and decided not to go. Sylvia was offered the open spot on the trip, and she jumped on it. "It was a trip, completely unintended, that changed my view of life forever. I have since been forever grateful for the richness of family and friends."

Susan Odegaard Turner got a surprise call from the governor's office asking if she'd be willing to take the first ever chief nurse executive position in the state prison system to set up a leadership team and oversee 5500 nurses. She said yes and did it for two years. It opened up a completely different specialty base of knowledge that is now part of what she consults about in her own business. "It was unexpected, serendipitous, divine intervention. Plus, I loved it!"

On an antiquing trip, Joyce bumped into a high school friend she hadn't seen in years. The friend happened to mention that her law office was looking for a receptionist. Joyce jumped in and reinvented herself as a legal secretary, which she's been doing for eighteen years now.

After a move, Charlene needed a job. She pulled into a parking lot to take a phone call, and when she hung up she realized she was parked in front of a bookstore. Spontaneously, she went inside and filled out an application. "Not only did I get a job, but I found a family of great friends and was no longer alone."

When she was a child, Karen would play library with her books, even stamping the due date inside with her very own date stamp. Years later, when she started thinking about going back to work, she contacted her local librarian. The librarian got back to her the next day, saying they'd just had some more hours approved, and would she like the job? "I was thrilled and have been working there ever since. It suddenly dawned on me that I'm actually doing the job I really wanted as a kid!"

As Joseph Campbell said, "Follow your bliss and doors will open where there were no doors before." Call it serendipity or synchronicity or divine intervention or luck or even karma. But whatever you call it, just make sure you walk through those doors!

CATITUDE

Before Jake and I head off to practice being foot-loose and fancy free again in a tiny tree house-like rental at the tip of Hilton Head, we notice a young cat in our front yard a few times. A beautiful calico cat, white with a sprinkling of beach pebble-like overlapping spots in black and ginger.

"Hi, sweetie," I say when it's close enough to hear me. The cat backs off a safe distance but doesn't run away. It looks clean and well fed, so we assume it's an outdoor cat from the neighborhood.

"How can people let their cats go outside?" we say. An outdoor cat's life expectancy is so much lower than that of an indoor cat. Hawks soar above our heavily treed neighborhood on a regular basis, and we've spotted coyotes wandering, one even strolling casually down the street at 10 A.M. There are always at least a few heartbreaking signs tacked to neighborhood telephone poles with pictures of cats and small dogs on them. *Roxie. Friendly 2-year-old female beagle/dachshund mix. Last seen 6-22. Please call 555-404-7777.*

When we arrive home after our beach trip, we see the cat almost immediately. And then we see it again. And again. And then one day, as I'm returning home from a walk, I see the cat slip into an impossibly small gap between one side of the front porch and the rough stone wall next to it.

It's actually an exaggeration to call it a front porch. It's really a long contemporary entryway stoop made of wood, the top maybe six inches off the ground. It's sheltered from the wind on one side by a wall and on the other by the way the house angles out, and the overhang of the roof shades it from the sun. I can't believe a small cat has managed to slip under it, and I'm sure there's no way it has enough room to stand up.

I stand there for a while, but it's my house and I kind of need to get into it. So eventually I walk over the porch to the door. The cat growls. I apologize.

The next time I go outside, the cat is gone. To make sure, I peer between the tiny gaps between the boards looking for a flash of white fur. I don't see one, but I'm almost sure I see a small shadow move. So I go inside to get Jake and a flashlight. Clumped into one corner we think we see what might or might not be a dirt-covered kitten. Or kittens. Or maybe it's a chipmunk. Or just dirt.

We go inside, and I open a can of tuna. Jake fills a bowl with water. We leave them both on the edge of the porch and go inside to peek out the windows. The cat is back in no time. That poor cat is so hungry. She devours the can of tuna, as well as all the cans of tuna that come after it. We switch to cat food. Now when I wake up early in the morning to write, she's sitting on the porch with a please feed me look in her eyes.

She eats, then she wiggles through the gap and under the porch, and then she comes back up and disappears for a while. We see definite kittens. We get glimpses of them through the gap in the side of the porch, and then one sunny day two of them venture out an inch or two to soak up some rays. They're usually in a cat pile and we can't get a clear enough glimpse for a count, but we think there might be three kittens, maybe four. When the mother's away, the biggest gingery orange kitten seems to be in charge and nudges the other kittens back under the porch if they poke their heads out too far.

We would happily stay like this forever, putting out cat food and trying to count dirt-covered kittens. But now it's November, and a cold snap is predicted a few nights away. The bravest kitten is venturing farther out from under the porch. Hawks have started circling overhead.

I Google and ask some experts. The consensus is that we should try to rescue the kittens when the mother is away. They're still young enough to be socialized and adopted. After the kittens are taken care of, we can borrow a trap from an animal rescue center, try to capture the mother, and then spay and release her. Since she's a feral, that's her best bet.

Separating the mother from her kittens is simply not an option for us. So we get together with our kids and hatch a plan. Saturday will be Operation Cat Rescue day. We'll start early and do whatever it takes.

I begin leaving dishes of cat food closer and closer to the front door. At the crack of dawn on Saturday morning, I tie a long rope to the door handle, then leave the door wide open and put a small amount of cat food just outside the door. I sit on a chair just inside the house and wait, an open cat carrier beside me on the floor. The mama cat hops up on the porch. She looks at me and hesitates. Then she eats and disappears.

Over the next few hours I set out more tiny amounts of cat food, closer to the open door, then on the threshold, then finally just inside the house. The poor hungry cat gobbles them up. But when I put a dish of food inside the open cat carrier, my brilliant plan being to shut the cat carrier door once she's inside, she gives me a *how stupid do you think I am?* look and takes off.

Our son and daughter and son-in-law are by their phones, on standby. Jake is hiding out in another part of the house. Since I've been doing most of the feeding, the mother cat is more comfortable around me.

Time is ticking. So I put the cat carrier out of sight and open my first can of Fancy Feast, which someone on the rescue message boards has called cat crack. I put the whole can in the bowl and set the bowl down just inside the house. I sit back down in my chair and grab the rope attached to the door handle.

The mother cat walks right in and goes straight for the cat crack. I know I have to do it, but making myself pull that rope is one of the hardest things I've ever done. The front door slams shut. She explodes in panic, scaling a tall window and snapping a slat of the heavy wooden blind with her force. She runs across the room, hurls her body at a glass door. She climbs another window, and then she tries to hide herself behind the contents of a built-in bookshelf, knocking treasures to the floor.

I don't know which one of us is more afraid. I want to let her back outside so I can stop shaking, but I know if I do, we'll never see her again. "Sorry," I whisper. "I'm really sorry, but it's going to be okay."

Per our plan, Jake has called the standby members of our team and then slipped out a back door to meet them. They have gloves, flashlights, cat treats, cat toys. It takes about an hour until Garet and her husband, Geoff, come in through the garage, the biggest ginger and white kitten in Garet's arms. She hands the kitten to me, and I place it on a blanket in a box in front the bookcase. Even now when I look at the pictures, the fear in those feline eyes, both mother's and baby's, breaks my heart.

The smaller ginger and white cat pokes its head out from under the porch to find out where the leader has gone, so they catch it right away. As I place the second kitten in the box next to the first one, I think the mother starts to realize that she isn't going to lose her kittens and relaxes a tiny bit.

We know there's at least one more kitten under there, but it has to be terrified by now, and even with a flashlight you can't see much under the porch. Finally, a little black and white kitten shows up in the gap beside the porch, and Garet manages to wedge her hand into the tiny space and reach it.

It's getting dark. And cold. There might or might not be another kitten under the porch. Kaden starts making detailed plans to demo the entire porch. Jake starts pacing back and forth. I stay inside, trying to calm the mama cat and her three kittens with fresh water and cat crack.

Garet sees movement under the porch. Geoff finds a piece of cardboard in the garage and cuts it to fit between the studs supporting the porch. He inserts the cardboard between the boards again and again and eventually nudges another panicked black and white kitten forward until Garet can grab it.

Twelve hours into a very long day, one mother cat and her four kittens, who have spent their entire lives up until now in a cramped dirty space under a porch, are safe. And they turn our entire lives upside down. There are long nights when the mother cat freaks out and starts crashing into windows again. But she's a good mom and she takes care of those kittens, and slowly she begins to trust us.

It might sound crazy, but after all they've been through, we think they deserve to stay together, so we keep them all. They stay with Jake and me until they're almost four months old, and then the two most outgoing kittens, (The Great) Catsby and Oreo, move up the street to live with Garet and Geoff and their other animals.

Mama cat, Pebbles, has learned to play now, and sometimes when she rolls around on the floor and thumps a stuffed bluebird with her hind legs, her kittens and best friends, Sunshine and Squiggy, just look at each other and shake their heads like the cooler-than-cool seven-month-old adolescents they are.

If our beloved dog Daisy had still been alive, crossing that porch several times a day on her way to or from a walk, Pebbles would have chosen another porch. I like to think Daisy sent us those kittens so we'd stop missing her so much and get over our stupid idea of never having another pet.

Every pet you say yes to leads you to the next pet. Every adventure you say yes to leads you to the next adventure. And if you keep your eyes open, something that could change your life in the best way could be hiding right underneath your front porch.

YOUR PLATFORM

The fog hasn't completely cleared, but your destination is starting to take shape. You've excavated that buried dream, and you're brushing it off and figuring out how to tweak it to get it to work for you. Or you've made your best guess on what you want to be when you grow up, at least for this reinvention, and you've fully committed to it.

You're continuing to jot down in your journal anything and everything you come across that might help you down the road—those ink-filled pages have some good information and a reassuring mass to them now. You've reached out for support and expert advice, and you might even have another passenger or two in your lifeboat.

Okay, so now you need a platform. I know how scary that sounds. It took me a while to even understand the concept. My first image was that a platform is a soapbox, and I was supposed to stand on top of it and hawk my books at the top of my lungs, like an old snake oil salesman. Fortunately for all of us, a platform is not a soapbox and it's not about selling.

A platform is something bigger than you and your particular reinvention. Think of it this way: You're driving down the road and you find the perfect beachy location to launch your reinvention. It's in a little sheltered bay, and there's even a floating dock with a ramp leading out to it. The dock is big enough to hold not just you, but all the people you come across who might like to hang out on this dock with you. And once those people climb aboard, they'll want to come back to visit as often as they can, not just because it's your dock, but because so many other fun, like-minded people spend time on it, too.

That dock is your platform. The people who hang out with you there are your peeps, your tribe, your supporters, your friends. I should probably pretend it came from a loftier place, but I once heard Keith Urban on *American Idol* quoting Nashville record producer Tony Brown as saying, "If you have a hit, you'll have an experience, but if you have an audience, you'll have a career." Your audience is on that platform.

Personally, I'm allergic to the word *fan* and never, ever use it. It feels like an insult to my readers, as if I think we're on different levels and I'm on a higher rung than they are. If anything, I am a fan of my readers, who give me the gift of this midlife career of mine, something I absolutely wouldn't have without them. I am grateful for them every day, which makes me want to share everything I can to support them in their own journeys.

One of my favorite examples is the waiting-for-the-school-bus platform. There's time to kill on that platform. Secrets are shared, advice is given, recommendations for everything from where to buy the freshest produce, to what movie is a total must-see, to whether or not you should get a new iPhone or switch to an Android, are shared. Some of the people on this platform might eventually form off-platform relationships, but it's just as likely that over the years they could give and gather all this support, even sharing intimate details of things like cancer and divorce, and never socialize outside of their waiting-for-the-school bus platform.

The three women in my novel *The Wildwater Walking Club* form a neighborhood-walking platform. Their lives are imploding, each in a different way, and they start getting together once a day to walk and talk and get themselves back on track. The support they give one another makes all the difference.

Say you're opening a restaurant. Your restaurant is not your platform. Your menu is not your platform. Your platform is the fact that your restaurant is cozy and welcoming, your staff is friendly and efficient, you cook with the freshest local ingredients, offer low carb choices, and feature local musicians, so that people who believe in and want these specific things know they can find them. Those people will become regulars and start chatting with the next table, exchanging recommendations for their favorite dishes on your menu. They'll begin to talk up your restaurant and send other people to it. *That's* your platform. The people who hang out on it with you keep your dream alive and thriving.

My platform is not my books. My platform is reinvention. Reinvention is the story of my life and my novels. It's something I believe in with all my heart, and something I think we all deserve, and can achieve, if we want it and we're willing to put in the hard work. I'm not only a total reinvention evangelist, meaning I talk up reinvention at every opportunity, but I also share everything I can to help others achieve their own reinventions. Reinvention is the thing that draws people not just to read my books, but to hang out with me on Facebook and Twitter and Pinterest and to visit ClaireCook.com and sign up for my newsletter.

My platform is absolutely a two-way street. I share things like reinvention tips, information about events and conferences, quotes, book excerpts, pictures and stories about my own adventures and even of my garden and cats. I do fun giveaways. But I invite my readers to share their own stories, too, and to provide details from their lives to help shape my books. *What would you like your life to be in five years and what's getting in your way? What's in your junk drawer?* This information, everything from dreams and obstacles to specific authentic details that I'd never be able to come up with on my own, is really valuable to me. But what's even more important is that it gives the people hanging out with me on my dock a chance to be a part of the conversation.

The real magic happens when this all takes on a life of its own. Suddenly side conversations are happening on my Facebook author page and I'm not even a part of them. Someone is using the platform I've provided to encourage somebody else, to cheer her on, or to say that she knows somebody else who just moved to

Seattle, too, and message her and she'd be happy to make the connection.

Okay, so I've been going back and forth about whether or not to add this next part. There are lots of people out there who will tell you never do this and always do that, but I try not to go down that road, because we're all so different and what makes sense for one person might not apply to another. But, I'm going to go out on a limb here, because I've seen so many people make this mistake, and I'd hate to see it impede your progress.

Connecting with others on another person's platform is not the same thing as jumping onto someone's platform to peddle your own stuff. If you didn't know that, that's okay, we all make mistakes, but it's a really uncool, rookie thing to do, so the sooner you learn that lesson the better things will go for you.

For instance, on my Facebook author page, I might ask, *What is the craziest thing that has happened to you this week?* Most people will share great stories, things that will make us all laugh or shake our heads. But there will always be one or two people who post something like, "I got an email from someone who loves my new book and just couldn't put it down and I wasn't expecting it so it was just the craziest thing, and by the way my book [INSERT BOOK TITLE HERE] is on sale at Amazon right now and here's the link . . .."

Highjacking another person's platform that way is not only rude, but it will most likely result in your comment being hidden or deleted by the dock owner. And even if it doesn't, everybody on that thread knows you've just done something tacky, which probably won't make you or your new book appealing to them. If instead you'd posted something interesting or helpful without being self-promoting, you might have genuinely connected with people who'd eventually want to know more about you and maybe even your book.

It's another thing entirely if you're invited to give a shout out for your Facebook page or your Twitter handle or your website or your book or your *whatever* on another person's platform. When that happens, jump on it!

I used to narrow my platform down a bit more and think of it as *midlife reinvention*, or even *reinvention for midlife women*. I do think that the majority of the people hanging out on my dock are midlife women. But reinvention can happen earlier, or later, and even many times throughout your life, and how exactly are we defining *midlife* these days anyway? The older I get, I can only imagine my own definition of midlife will just keep expanding to include me. I mean, who wants to be in the endlife category?

Once I was signing stock at a bookstore while I was on book tour. A bookseller in her twenties came up to me and said, "You might think it's weird that I read all your books, but I like finding out what the rest of my life will be like." It was such a great comment. I'd never thought of it that way before, but it made me realize I'd instinctively made my novels multi-generational, because in a way they're about the continuum of our experiences.

I've also received some wonderful emails from women telling me that they like to read my books and then share them with both their daughters and their mothers. The thought of three generations of women in one family reading my books is just the best thing ever.

So I've broadened my platform to just *reinvention*. If you think you belong on my dock and you want to hang out there, especially if you're a nice person and you like to have fun, then hop aboard! I've come to think that, rather than putting too fine a point on it, it's better to step back a bit and let my platform be self-selecting. I don't want to make the call about who fits and who doesn't. That's your call. Midlife women or younger or older. Reinventors or reinventors-to-be. Those few good men I mentioned earlier. Or just people who like reading fun beach books, whether they read them at an actual beach, by a lake, next to a pool, or in the bathtub. You're all invited. Jump on, there's plenty of room. I'd love to have you.

And also feel free to hop off if you're not feeling it. That part's self-selecting, too. Don't hang around, sighing and rolling your eyes, trying to melt our chill, or even to try to get us to renovate the dock to your specifications. There are plenty of other docks out there, so go find one that's a better fit, one that will support and inspire you and let you do the same for others.

HOW NOT TO BE A DINOSAUR

If you're holding your head because I've just given you a platform headache, if you can't even begin to imagine how you'd accomplish this platform thing for your own reinvention, take a deep breath and bear with me.

Before we get into the details, one of the biggest pieces of advice I have for you is to get your tech together. When I say this in a workshop, about a third of the participants either look away or get that deer-in-the-headlights look. And these are the people I'm talking to. So even if you really, really don't want to read this section, make yourself read it anyway.

You can access all, or at least most, of the information you need to get where you're going just by tapping your keyboard. And because our world is changing at such lightning speed, if you don't figure out how to do this, the sad but true fact is that you could be a dinosaur in no time.

I know how intimidating this can be. What helped me was that, back in my teaching days, all the teachers at my school were given a summer assignment to find a computer mentor and get up to speed. There is nothing like having someone who is willing to sit down with you at a computer and answer even your most embarrassing questions. *Uh, where exactly is the On switch on this thing?* (A big thank you to Rita Speroni for being my computer mentor all those years ago!)

If you need a computer mentor, find one. Ask a friend. Hire the twelve-year-old down the street. Take a class at your community center. If the first attempt doesn't give you what you need, try someone or something else.

In a nutshell, what you have to do is get to a place where you realize you don't have to know it all. Nobody knows it all. You simply have to acquire enough knowledge, and be comfortable enough, so that you can figure out the finite number of things you need to know to do the handful of things you need to do. To learn not be afraid to try things. To realize that the computer will not blow up if you guess wrong.

A big revelation for me came from my son Kaden. He majored in interactive game design in college and has a graduate certification in health Internet technology. He worked in the video game industry until that field took a nosedive and then, at the ripe old age of twenty-six, he reinvented himself as a build engineer for a digital advertising company.

Once he was telling me about some high drama difficulties they'd had on a big release. "How did you figure it out?" I asked.

He shrugged. "We Googled it."

Up until that point I think I'd just assumed that these genius IT people had all the answers. Who knew they actually track them down the way mere mortals like the rest of us do. It was like being in kindergarten and running into your teacher at the grocery store and being bowled over that Ms. Jones *eats*.

I've learned to Google everything I need to know. Best of all, there is a video out there on how to do practically anything under the sun, from getting started on Twitter, to getting rid of the background on a photo with Photoshop Elements, to fixing your running toilet. You don't have to conceptually understand how to do these things—you just have to find the right video. Google it up. Or go to YouTube and do a search. Once you've found a video that works for you, watch the first step. Pause the video and do it. Move on to the next step, pause the video, do it. And the next and the next until you've finished your project.

I've accomplished so much this way, from learning about metadata and SEO, to creating banners for my website and social media profile pages. I bookmark the videos so I'll be able to find them the next time I need this information. For backup, I jot a note to myself in one of my notebooks, writing down the title I've used for the bookmark. Not having to memorize the steps or actually learn how to do these things really takes the pressure off.

KEEPING YOUR
PLATFORM AFLOAT

By the time I finish writing this section, something I've written could have changed. The next big thing might happen tomorrow or the next day, and we'll all be scurrying to climb onboard. Or Facebook could jump the shark and become the next MySpace, and we'll all be taking down our pages, shaking our heads and mumbling to ourselves, "What was I *thinking?*"

It's important to remember that even though these specifics will inevitably change, the *process* of building your platform and keeping it afloat will remain the same. You'll keep your eyes and ears open to stay current, and Google up the latest information when you need it. I'll be doing the same thing at my end, and I'll update specific information if it starts to make this book feel dinosaurish. I'll let everybody know I've done that via my website and newsletter and other parts of my own platform, like Facebook and Twitter, or wherever we're all hanging out then.

YOUR WEBSITE

Okay, let's get going. I think of my website, ClaireCook.com, as my platform hub. It's the most reliable place to find me, and my hope is that everyone I meet or who reads my books will go there and take advantage of all the free stuff: information about reinvention and writing, excerpts of my books, event info, speaker info, giveaways, my blog. I also really hope you'll sign up for my free newsletter while you're there, because that makes it a two-way street—you can reach me, but I can also reach out to you to let you know about a new release or special offer or giveaway or event, or fingers crossed, even another movie.

I don't exist only on my website. I spend time out in the real world, speaking at events and meeting people at the park or the grocery store or at the dentist's office. And I spend time in the virtual world, too, on Facebook and Twitter and Pinterest and doing the occasional interview or guest post on somebody else's website or blog.

And as much as I love doing these things just for the sake of doing them (except maybe the dentist and the grocery store), I also hope that the people I happen to connect with will be interested enough to go to my website and check out the information I share and sample my books. If they like what they see, if it feels like the right click, I hope they'll sign up for my newsletter, too. That way, if I never see them again at the park, or if Twitter becomes soooo last year, we can still hang out together.

Because it's my hub, my website address is on everything. My books. My business cards. My email signature. My social networking profiles. My website address is also mentioned in my bio on anything I might write for a magazine or a blog. ClaireCook.com is the place everything else points to.

Just this morning, I actually did go to the dentist: A new dental assistant asks me what I do for a living. I tell her I'm a writer, she asks for more details, and then she says she's a huge reader. We go back and forth while she tries to figure out if she's read any of my novels, and then I tell her a little bit about this book-to-be. She follows me out to the reception room, writing my website address on a Post-It and asking me which book she should read first. "Skim through the excerpts on my website," I say. "One will call out to you. And make sure you sign up for my newsletter so I can let you know when the reinvention book will be out."

Imagine how much more complicated this might have been if I didn't have a hub to send her to. If I'd sent her to Amazon, she might have felt like I was hard-selling my books to her. If I'd sent her to my Facebook or Twitter page, she wouldn't have immediately found what she was looking for, and then she might well have clicked on somebody's pet pig video and forgotten all about me and my books.

So, give your reinvention a hub and make it easy to find. The best way to do this is to create your own website hosted on your own domain. (If you're a blogger, your blog can live on that site.) Essentially you're going to create an online home base, which will be the place everyone can find you no matter what becomes hot—or not—in the world of social networking. If you're looking for me and you Google Claire Cook, as I just did a moment ago, ClaireCook.com is the first of a whopping 39,700,000 results that come up.

I paid about $99 to buy ClaireCook.com for ten years, and when the time ran out, I renewed it for another ten for about the same price. You can buy your domain for a year at a time instead, or at intervals in between the two. You'll also need to hire a website hosting service to keep your site uploaded on the Internet. I pay less than $10 a month for that. You can buy your domain first and then look around for your hosting service, or you can find the website hosting service and let them help you buy your domain for a small charge. Some of the hosting services even include one free domain name as well as a free site-builder.

I'd be happy to share my own specifics, but the truth is I'm not even sure the choices I made are the best ones. I just know that they gave me what I needed at a price I was happy with, and I wanted to give you some ballpark numbers so you'd have a reference point as you look around. But I just asked my Facebook and Twitter friends which hosts they're using that they're happy with. Hostgator, Bluehost, iPage, and FatCow were some of the names that came back, if you're looking for a few to compare. There are plenty of good options and some great deals out there, so just Google up how to buy a domain and best website hosts to get some expert advice.

Once you own your address and have a host, you'll need a website to put up there. You can hire someone to build your website for you, or you can build one yourself. Or if your host offers a free site builder, you can use that.

If you want a clean site with great functionality, WordPress is a terrific option. Just Google up some free Wordpress website tutorials. Katrina of 77webstudio.com is my personal favorite. She's a talented teacher, and I just rebuilt my website with the help of one of her step-by-step videos. She offers a free Create Your Wordpress Website video course on her website, as well as a variety of videos on her 77webstudio YouTube channel, like the one I used. You can also hire her to build your website.

One thing that confused me in the beginning was the difference between WordPress.com and Word-Press.org. If you don't want to spend money on your own domain or host, you can build your site/blog at WordPress.com and they'll host it online for you for free. But, and it's a big but, you won't have a direct address like ClaireCook.com, which is going to make it harder for people to find you. (Your address will be YourReinvention.WordPress.com.) In order to have your own direct address, as I said above, you'll also have to find a website hosting service and buy your own domain. Then you'll download WordPress from Word-Press.org or from a direct download link your new web hosting service provides. If you can afford the invest-ment, I think it's money well spent. If you can't, you can always start at Wordpress.com and move your site over to your own address when you're ready.

There are lots of other options out there for easy template-based website building, including a software program called Sandvox if you're on a Mac, and if you don't mind a monthly fee, Squarespace also makes it easy to build a sleek, professional website. But Word-Press is the top dog, and because the majority of web-sites are now designed with it, you'll have no trouble finding the information and support you need.

I think building your own website can be incredibly empowering, and because there are so many great tem-plates available, you don't have to know HTML—or even what it is! If you build your site yourself, you'll know how to make changes to keep it fresh, instead of having to hire, and pay, your web designer every time you want to add something new. When you do it your-self, you can keep tweaking and tweaking until it truly reflects your personality and the platform feel you're going for. And any time you want a new look, you can just change the theme or template yourself.

Sure, there's a learning curve, but experimenting with templates and themes and photos and fonts and color is creative and fun. If at some point you need functionality that you can't figure out on your own—

say an online store—you can always hire out for just that piece of it.

If doing it yourself doesn't sound the least bit appealing, and you can afford it, by all means hire someone. Shop around. Find websites like the one you want and scroll down to the bottom to see who designed them. Google up some WordPress website designers and send them to the sites you like and ask them how much it would cost to create something like that.

What you want is a professional looking, easy-to-navigate site that has the right look for your platform. It needs to feel alive and have fresh content added often enough to keep people coming back to hang out. I've seen lots of gorgeous websites that never change—once you've been there, there's no reason to ever stop back again, and you're likely to find lots of outdated info on them, too. Your hub needs to be maintained so it doesn't start to look like a ghost town. So even if you hire someone else to design it, make sure they show you how to change content yourself. If they're not willing to do that, look for another designer.

YOUR EMAIL LIST

Make sure your website includes a really visible place for visitors to leave their names and email addresses so that it becomes a two-way street. That way, you'll be able to reach out to them, too—with a coupon for your catering business, an invitation to your grand opening, or a regular newsletter. Again, you don't need to reinvent the wheel on this—check out the websites of other people in your field and see how they do it. Sign up for their email lists and see what they send you. When you find something you admire, use it as a jumping off point and then add your own unique twist.

I've made many, many mistakes along the way, but one of the smartest things I've done is to build a great email list. This means I can reach my tribe/peeps/readers directly, which is huge. It can even be one of the biggest components of a successful reinvention.

Building an email list is a brick-by-brick kind of thing. First, I'd suggest that you find an email service to manage your list for you. Some of them will do it for free until your list grows to a certain size—for instance, MailChimp is free for lists of up to 2,000. If you have a big list and don't send out lots of email, you can choose a service that will only charge you when you send something out—MailChimp and CampaignMonitor have pay-as-you-go options.

If you're going to be sending frequent emails, you might want to check out services that charge you a monthly fee for unlimited sending, like AWeber and ConstantContact. You can Google up lots of other choices, too. What you're looking for is a service that manages your list for you, makes it easy to create sign-up forms for your website, has professional looking, customizable templates that will give your emails the look you want, has good deliverability (meaning the email you send won't bounce) as well as easy one-click sending, and provides analytics you can understand so you'll know how many people are actually opening whatever you send.

Once you choose an email service, if you have any trouble figuring things out after you've read the instructions and Googled up tutorials, contact support. If they won't walk you through it, you might want to consider another company.

When your sign-up form is on your website, and your reinvention is up and running to the point that you're ready to start collecting people for that platform of yours, it's time to start building your email list.

Never, ever buy an email list, even if the pitch is that the list is targeted or verified or *whatever*. The best that can happen is you'll be out some money and end up with random people on your list. The worst is that you'll get dumped by your email service because so many of these "verified" emails bounce.

I suggest that you make a list of all the people you can think of that might want to support you in your reinvention, as well as the people you know that might be interested in your soon-to-open salvage warehouse or just-launched podcast. Send them each an individual email if you can, telling them about your new project and how excited and nervous you are, and asking them to support you by going to your website to check it out and joining your email list to stay in the loop.

You'll get a much better response with individual emails, but if you absolutely can't find the time, send a group email. But do it the right way: Send it to yourself and put all the recipients in the BCC field to keep them from being visible, so you're not inadvertently sharing private email addresses or calling attention to the fact that this message is going out to everybody you can think of and not just a few of your dearest friends.

Do not skip this step and just start adding people to your email list without their permission. The spam police have really tightened up on this sort of thing, and doing that is actually illegal now. People tagging your newsletter/announcement as spam is another good way to get dumped by your email service.

If you share valuable and interesting information and give the people on your email list things that are just for them—an early book excerpt, a coupon, a sneak peek photo—they'll want to stay on your email list. We're all busy and we all have too much email to read, so don't be boring, and don't send anything out unless you have something to say.

Giveaways can be a great incentive to get people to take the time to sign up for your list. You can put a giveaway right on your website: A picture of the prize, with a caption that says *Sign up for my newsletter for a chance to win* with an email list sign-up form right below. If your reinvention involves a brick and mortar place, you can also set up a physical giveaway right as you walk in the door. As long as you make it clear that they're signing up for your newsletter, you can ask them to leave their names and email addresses on a sheet of paper and then you can add them to your list, or if you want to be extra safe, your sign can send them to your website. They can pull out their smartphones or tablets right there to sign up.

As for giveaway prizes, be careful. I think the best prizes are things that would only appeal to the people who would want to be on your list anyway. For instance, I give away mostly signed and personalized books—sometimes a beach bag filled with signed copies of all my books. If you're not a reader or you don't like my books, then the prize (with the possible exception of the beach bag) is not going to appeal to you.

So if you want an email list that has real value because it's composed of people who want to hang out on your platform with you, don't give away a car. Or anything that would appeal to everybody under the sun. The people who aren't into what you're doing might well unsubscribe to your list when they find out they haven't won anyway, so it's wasted effort all around.

Also, how sad would it be if a random person you'll never see again were to win your really great prize. So much better to make the day of one of your deserving supporters, and a good giveaway choice can make the odds of that happening much higher.

The best thing you can do as you grow your list is to keep it real.

THE SOCIAL NETWORKING DANCE

Social media might seem to be about the technology, but it's really about the connections. Networking through social media, or social networking, is a terrific way to spread the word about your reinvention and to meet other reinventors. You can also connect with others in your specific field, as well as find people who will help keep your dream alive and thriving. So many new readers have discovered my novels via the magic of social networking. Lots of opportunities have come to me that way, too, things that simply wouldn't have happened any other way.

Social media can be amazingly powerful and lots of fun, but it can also be a total time suck. If you're spending all your time on Facebook, you're probably not getting much closer to your reinvention destination. I mentioned this earlier, but I think it bears repeating that my trick is to finish my two pages a day before I allow myself to check email or Facebook or Twitter.

It you hate social networking, it will show, so don't do it. But before you decide to abstain, give it a chance. Make sure you really hate it and you're not just intimidated by it. There's a real learning curve—it's like entering a new world at first—but it doesn't take long until it gets easier. And before you know it, you'll be an old pro and might even start enjoying yourself. When you get stuck along the way or if some new change throws you, support is just a Google search away.

I've already given one example of this, but it's crucial to remember that social networking is not about selling. If you follow someone on Twitter and they're kind enough to follow you back, do not immediately tweet them a message asking them to buy your CD, watch your YouTube video, contribute to your Indiegogo campaign, or babysit your kids. It's rude and inappropriate.

I think of social networking as a dance. The best partners are graceful and courteous and charming and generous, and they work hard not to step on toes. What funny or helpful or inspiring things can you share while you're dancing? How can you help and encourage the other dancers? If you spend most of your time doing these things, if you like and share and retweet for others, then when you have something special to talk up, there's plenty of accumulated goodwill and people will be open to hearing it.

Oh, just in case you don't already know this, never use all capital letters—PEOPLE WILL THINK YOU'RE YELLING AT THEM!

FACEBOOK

One of the most valuable social networking vehicles for me has been Facebook, and I think it's a great place to start. There are many valid ways to approach Facebook to support your reinvention. I'll share what I've done, not because I think it's the only way, or necessarily the best way for you, but to give you a jumping off point for your own approach.

Once I'd signed up for Facebook and filled out my profile and posted a few photos and other things, I began to invite people to be my friends as I noticed they were on Facebook. Old friends, new friends, my readers, relatives, former classmates, people I didn't know but whose work I admired—writers of all kinds, musicians, entrepreneurs, artists, and other reinventors. I also accepted friend requests from anyone who didn't look sketchy, though I always clicked through to their profile page to check them out first.

Some people I know will only send friend invitations or accept friend requests from people they actually know in the physical world. The way I look at friendship, virtual and otherwise, is the more the merrier, and I love connecting with all these interesting new people. (Although the downside of having lots of friends on Facebook is that your feed gets so busy you miss most of the things they post.)

Other people I know divide their friends into lists, and then filter their posts so that certain things they say only go out to certain lists. Just thinking about doing that makes me tired, and I can't even imagine taking the time to figure out which list should get what. So my rule of thumb is that I just don't post anything I wouldn't be comfortable with the whole wide world reading. There's lots of oversharing on Facebook, so the fact that you'll never read about the fight I had with my husband (not that we fight!) or see my wild party pics (ha!) is probably not a huge loss.

Facebook allows you to have 5,000 friends. When you're just starting out and you have exactly three friends, that can seem like a pie-in-the-sky number. But once you start spending a little bit of time every day or so connecting and building on Facebook, your friend tally will add up.

When my friend count got up to about 3,000, I set up my Facebook author page and invited all my friends to like it. Many of them did. And pretty quickly lots of new people, who might not have been comfortable sending me a friend request since we don't know each other in the real world, found my page and liked it. There is definitely overlap—people who are my friends and have also liked my page—but there are also people who are either one or the other. I do most of my posting on my author page now, since there are substantially more people there, and because I don't want to make people feel spammed by double posting. But it's good to know that for a special announcement, I have two ways to reach out on Facebook.

Some people prefer not to set up a Facebook page, or as Facebook calls it, a Page. Instead they enable their original Facebook profile to allow people to follow them. There's no limit to the number of followers you can have, so once you run out of space for friends, people who friend you will automatically become followers. For me, the concept of follower feels too close to fan, which I hate, so I've chosen not to go this route, and so far my author page has worked out really well. But things change often on Facebook, so I'll keep my eyes and ears open and readjust when I need to.

If your name is not directly tied to your reinvention, a Facebook page in the name of your salvage warehouse or vacation house-sitting business would obviously make more sense for you than enabling followers on your personal profile. But early on, I made the mistake of starting a separate page for one of my novels. Lots of people were kind enough to jump aboard and like it. But then I went on to the next novel, and I suddenly realized what a nightmare it would be to try to manage a separate page for each of my books—I'd be up to twelve by now! At that point I started my Facebook author page in my own name. It took a considerable amount of work to get the word out to people to leave my book page and join me there, and I'm sure I lost some stragglers along the way.

So, if this applies to you, learn from my mistake. If it doesn't apply, make sure you look around to see what other like-minded reinventors in your field are doing before you decide on your approach.

There are lots of good Facebook tutorials out there, and you can also do a search right on Facebook to get started. Once you're up and running, make sure you like my Facebook author page. You can send me a friend request, too, if I haven't yet reached my Facebook-imposed friend limit, as long as you don't mind that I don't post there very often.

When and if you decide to start your own Facebook page, if you post the link to it on my page, along with a nice comment, I'd be more than happy to like your page for you. Other eyes will see your post, too, and might well follow suit. There are lots of kind and supportive people, many of them reinventors themselves, hanging out on my author page!

You can also start your own Facebook group, either a public or private or a secret group, and invite your Facebook friends with a shared interest. And you're cordially invited to join the private Facebook group I've recently started for reinventors. Just go to Facebook.com/groups/NeverTooLateReinvention and click Join Group.

TWITTER

From the beginning, Facebook felt pretty instinctive to me. It was like chatting with a group of people at a cookout or a cocktail party, without the hassle of having to decide what to wear or put on makeup first. Just the way it is at a party, many other conversations were going on at once, but a group of us were all on one thread, having one conversation.

Based on my Facebook experience, I fully expected to enjoy Twitter. So I was completely surprised when it was hate at first sight. The noise was deafening. Rather than being able to engage in a single conversation, it felt like everybody was standing alone and shouting at the top of their lungs. And nobody was listening. And those silly hashtags—#OMG. #WTF. Twitter not only didn't feel intuitive to me, it didn't seem to have anything to do with actually connecting with other human beings. And every time I saw #amwriting, I would think, yep, that's exactly what I should be doing right now instead of wasting my time on Twitter.

But I hung in there, and soon I was having real, if very short, conversations. Women who were already reading my books started reaching out to me, saying nice things about them and asking when my next one was coming out. I connected with loads of interesting new people there, too, and it turned out to be a great place to spread the word about events and ask questions. A surprising number or invitations for interviews and speaking gigs began to come my way via Twitter.

You can get up and running on Twitter easily with one of the many tutorials out there. Your Twitter handle, or username, is important. Instead of going for something witty or creative, it will help your visibility to use your name or the name of your blog or other reinvention, and it's ideal to match this to your website address as well as your other social media addresses.

Unfortunately, I waited too long to jump on the Twitter bandwagon to be able to get my own name. It turned out there are quite a few Claire Cooks in the world, and one of the others got there first, though she spends a fair amount of time forwarding tweets my way, so maybe one day she'll decide to throw in the towel and give me our name. In the meantime, I'm @ClaireCookwrite on Twitter. It's not perfect, but I've also used this handle on Pinterest and a few other places, so it's fine.

It's also really important to have a good Twitter profile bio. Rather than going for cute or pithy, I think it's far better to be authentic. I get compliments on my bio all the time, not because it's brilliant, but because it tells you exactly who I am and what my platform is. Another author kindly tweeted this to me recently: *Catchy #author profile. One of the best I've seen.*

As soon as you read my bio, you know right away whether you're in or you're out, whether you want to follow me or not. I also hope my bio might inspire you in your own life. Just in case it's helpful as a jumping off point, as I'm writing this my bio reads: *Wrote 1st novel in minivan at 45. Walked red carpet w/ MUST LOVE DOGS at 50. Now bestselling author of 11 novels & reinvention book on the way. Midlife rocks!*

Never, ever buy Twitter followers, and I don't think using programs to auto-follow people is a productive way to go either. But the good news is that, with a strong bio and a welcoming profile picture, it's pretty easy to build a Twitter following. My technique is that, when I have a bit of extra time, I do a topical search on Twitter—say, reinvention—or I might pull up the Twitter followers of a blog I enjoy whose readers might tweet things I'd be interested in reading and sharing, and who might also enjoy my books down the road. Then I just scroll through their list of followers, scan their bios, and let the right people jump out at me. When they do, I click Follow.

If they don't follow me back in a week or so, or whenever I find the time to notice, I take it to mean they're not that into me, so I just unfollow them. There are lots of free programs out there, like Tweeter Karma, which will pull up all the people you're following at once so you can see if they're following you back. They'll also let you see if you've missed following anyone you want to follow. I admit this is something I don't find the time to do very often, but it's nice to know it's an option.

When new people follow me on Twitter, I take a quick peek at their profile picture to make sure they're wearing clothes and/or don't look like escaped convicts. If their picture is creepy or just the default Twitter egg, I don't follow back, especially since they might be some kind of spambot, a web robot that could try to hack into my account or spread a virus or whatever else spambots do these days.

If this person passes my profile pic screening, I take a quick look at her bio. If there isn't one, I won't follow back, again because I don't know who she is. If she does have a bio, but it's obnoxious or offensive or appears to be all about selling something, I'll pass. And while I follow back just about everyone else, a good bio might make me want to know more about that person, and then if I have time I'll click on the link—to their hub!

It's not a perfect system. I have lots of Twitter followers now, and sometimes I miss following someone back. If I accidentally do that to you, just retweet something I've tweeted or tweet me a nice message, and I'll check to see if I'm following you, and if not, I will. That's a far more effective way of doing the Twitter dance than tweeting, as someone once did to me: *Hey, I followed you three hours ago. How come you're not following me back yet?* Uh, because I have a life?

There are people on Twitter who think it's cool to have five gazillion followers and only follow seven people. Again, that feels too much like the fan thing to me, and an insult to the people who are kind enough to follow me. So I make following on Twitter a two-way street. The downside is that if you're following seven people, you can see everything they post, but if you're following lots more, your Twitter feed is insanely busy and you can't possibly read all the tweets.

If you're a list person, you can solve this by creating Twitter lists of people whose tweets you don't want to miss. Or you can do what I do: just don't worry about it. If someone wants to make sure I see their tweet, it's as easy as including @ClaireCookwrite in it so that it will show up in my notifications.

A word about direct (private) messages on Twitter, and on Facebook, too. I've stopped reading them. It simply got to be too much, and reading them, let alone trying to respond to them all, began to encroach on my writing time.

So here's how I do it now: If you post on my Facebook author page or tweet something to me, I'll make every effort to respond. The bonus is that if it's a question about reinvention or writing or one of my books or an upcoming event, both the question and answer will be public and might benefit others, which keeps the social in social networking. If it's something that warrants a private message, I hope you'll take the time to send me an email through my website. Sometimes it takes me a while to work through my inbox, but I do my best to answer every email.

It was hard for me to make the decision to limit my availability a bit, but it was also a good reminder that we all need to make social networking work for us and not against us. So if you start to feel overwhelmed, take some time to come up with an approach that works for you.

I've made many wonderful and surprising connections on Twitter. One of my best Twitter dance stories so far happened like this: After I finish writing my pages one day, I turn my attention to Twitter. I check my notifications and respond to everyone who has mentioned me in a tweet. Then I take a moment to glance at my feed, looking for something interesting or helpful to retweet.

A tweet from @KathyCaprino catches my eye. I've never met Kathy and I don't even know how we started following each other on Twitter, but her tweet promises tips for writers who hope to engage readers and has a link to a piece she's written for Forbes.com. Her tweet also calls the link to the attention of the person she interviewed for the article by including her twitter handle at the end.

I click on the link to see if it's something my Twitter followers might enjoy. Kathy has done a terrific interview with Amy Newmark, who reinvented her life in 2008 by buying the Chicken Soup for the Soul publishing company from its founders, Jack Canfield and Mark Hansen, with her husband and a group of investors. Amy's advice for writers and speakers, from using the power of storytelling, to focusing on the positive, to making sure you're passionate about your subject, is so spot on that I read every word. As soon as I've finished, I tweet this, along with the link to the story: *So true! @kathycaprino 7 tips 4 writers who hope 2 engage millions of readers via @Forbes @ForbesWoman @amynewmark.*

Amy, who has clearly read my Twitter bio first, reaches out to me to say they're planning a book called *Reboot Your Life* and that I should be in it, and she asks me if I would write a story for them.

My blinders are on and I'm deeply into writing this book, and I also have two novels on the backburner, a sequel to *The Wildwater Walking Club* and Book 3 of the *Must Love Dogs* series. So I respond, thanking Amy so much for thinking of me and telling her I'm too focused on my own books right now to add another project.

But because there's such synchronicity to the timing of her invitation—I'm writing my first nonfiction book about reinvention at the exact same time she asks me to contribute to a nonfiction book about reinvention—I can't resist adding that what intrigues me are the cross-promotion possibilities.

Let's talk, Amy responds. And so we do. And by the end of a fabulous conversation, Amy has asked me to coauthor *Reboot Your Life* with her. I'll write the introduction as well as a story, and help narrow down and edit the thousands of story submissions they've received to a total of 101. What I have to offer is my reinvention platform and my passion for the subject. *Chicken Soup for the Soul* has oodles of loyal readers, who I hope will discover my books through this collaboration. It's a total win-win, and I'm so glad it worked out.

And it all started with a simple tweet. I wasn't trying to get anything. I was simply retweeting something to help another writer and to share valuable information with the writers who follow me.

Call it synchronicity, serendipity, or the Twitter dance. But whatever you call it, it absolutely demonstrates the magic of social networking. And proves once again that karma really is a boomerang!

SOCIAL MEDIA OVERLOAD

There are lots and lots of other social networking options, but if you use them all, you'll never have time for anything else. Which is great if your dream is to become a social media maven, but for the rest of us, not so much. Just the way choosing one thing and pouring all your passion and energy into it ups your chances for success, choosing a limited number of social media options and doing them well is much more likely to produce the results you're looking for than spreading yourself too thin.

I wish I had more time to devote to Pinterest, because I think playing with pictures on boards instead of words on a page for a change is both soothing and fun. If my reinvention had anything to do with design or food, I'd find the time for Pinterest. LinkedIn is important in the business world, but it's too buttoned up to be my thing, so I have a tiny presence there, basically to tell people where else they can find me.

Google+, YouTube, Instagram, or Tumblr might make sense for you, or they might not. Visit the websites of some people in your reinvention field. If they're active on social media, you'll see a row of little social media icons on their homepage that will tell you which ones they're using. You can click through to find out how they're using these sites and to figure out whether or not they might be beneficial to you.

Just remember that your ultimate goal in social media, beyond making genuine connections with people and not burning yourself out, is to send everybody who's interested in finding out more about you and your reinvention to your hub. Make sure you have a link to your website, in the most visible place you can put it, in all of your social media profiles, from Facebook to Twitter to anywhere else you decide to venture.

But again, don't let social media take over your life. Set a timer if you need to!

GETTING UNSTUCK

So, where are you now? Have you chosen your destination? Are you cruising along Reinvention Road? Sunglasses on, radio blaring, A/C blasting, figuring out your route as you go? Feeling a little bit more like the person you were meant to be every day?

Are you doing your version of my two pages a day, moving forward step-by-step, day in and day out? Have you found a way to make yourself accountable? Are you using your notebook to jot down everything that might come in handy down the road? Keeping an eye out for the right passengers for your lifeboat? Thinking about your platform and beginning to build it, one brick at a time?

If so, that's great. Pat yourself on the back because you are absolutely on your way. Keep chugging along, and remember some days will be much harder than others, but you'll have amazing days, too, days when everything starts to click.

If you're stuck, let's try to figure out why. I just took another look at the posts from my Facebook research assistants about what they want their lives to be in five years and what's standing in their way. Some of these obstacles might be exasperating, but, with persistence, they're conquerable: *Having my own classroom is my goal. I have to retake a communications class I have taken 3 times! I need a straight B and I keep getting a B-*, one woman posts. How incredibly frustrating, but hang in there! And if you haven't tried it yet, maybe you should ask the professor to let you submit an extra credit assignment. Or ask someone who's aced the class to tutor you for the final exam.

Other obstacles are more treacherous: *Commitment to the family business my parents own. I work for my brother who will inherit the business. I would love to be beachfront reading books and doing yoga for a living, but that is just fantasy.* Okay, let me get this straight. You're devoting your one and only life to the family business, and you're not even going to inherit a share of it? And if you really want to live close enough to a beach to read books there, why does that have to be a fantasy? And why can't you start working toward at least partially supporting yourself by teaching yoga? Just tell your brother the boss you'll be leaving early on Tuesdays and Thursdays to get certified/teach a yoga class. If he freaks out and fires you, you're free, free at last!

Someone else posts this: *I've always felt that I needed permission from others to do what I wanted.* Another woman writes: *Other people's expectations.*

These comments make me remember a conversation on Isla Mujeres. "I'm really good at following the rules," Jen says when we chat about her life at the We Move Forward conference. She clearly has talent and energy and dreams, but she can't seem to allow herself to go there.

I think it's important to ask yourself if your need to get permission or fulfill other people's expectations or follow the rules is an excuse. If what's really going on is that you're afraid to take the first step, and hanging onto this obstacle with all your might keeps you from having to push past that fear.

Also, the truth is these *other people* might well be so focused on their own lives that they won't even notice you've stepped out of the box until you're well on your way to finally doing what you've always wanted to do. And, really, in the scheme of things, what's a little disapproval? If you're going after a dream you love, you'll be too busy to spend much time noticing it anyway.

Don't ask, just do it. Once your idea has incubated and you're far enough down the road that your dream has started to take on a life of its own, you can casually start to fill everybody in. It might not have to be a big deal if you don't make it one.

Some more Facebook posts about what's standing in the way: *My children. Full time job. I can't walk away from my day job. Three kids. Family obligations. Keeping everyone else afloat. Tricky family issues. A family member's mental health. Family obligations. Demanding boss. Family obligations. Family obligations.*

I get it. In all of our lives, there will always, always be something. As Dorothy Parker once answered the ringing phone that had interrupted her work, "What fresh hell is this?"

It's so easy to let these never-ending, perfectly legitimate demands on your time eat up your life. And suddenly you have a bad case of helper's disease—you help everyone but yourself. Or you turn into a martyr, which is great if your dream is to be canonized as a saint someday, but otherwise, not so much. Poor me. Look how I give and give. Okay, I'll do that for you, sigh, even though I was planning to use the time to start reinventing my life.

As we used to say when we were kids, *Do you want a medal or a chest to pin it on?* Martyr syndrome gets you nowhere. And it's really just one great big excuse.

Excuses. They're out there. As many as you might ever want or need.

If I sound less than sympathetic, it's because writing this section is giving me major flashbacks to my own pre-reinvention days. I did it all. The excuses. The martyr bit. Everybody else's needs. I didn't realize I was doing it at the time, but looking back I can see that I used my family and my jobs and everything else I could come up with as excuses. I kept myself ridiculously busy because I was afraid if I had any extra time, I might have to look at the fact that I'd chickened out on living the life I was born to live. I think I was showing off a little, too—how capable I was, how nice I was, how many balls I could juggle at once. But bottom line, it was a smokescreen so I didn't have to face that book I was oh, so terrified to write.

I'm not at all suggesting we shirk our responsibilities or stop supporting the people we love. If my husband or kids need me, I'm there. If they need me but it's not desperate, I'm there after I finish today's pages. If they don't really need me, they've learned to respect my time enough to wait until I've finished writing. When my kids were younger and I was teaching at one school and consulting for two others, I did the writing-in-my-minivan thing. You don't need every waking hour to reinvent your life. Slow and steady use of those tiny pockets of time you have available to you can get you there.

But I've also learned to separate the important demands on my time from the ones I can let go, the ones that really aren't that essential in the scheme of things. Or that someone else will handle if I don't jump immediately. Doing this frees up big chunks of my time for work that matters to me. It's amazing how someone else will figure out how to grocery shop if there's no food in the house. I've also come to believe life is too short to worry about a clean house, so I neither feel guilty nor look at it as just my problem when mine gets messy. Living in yoga pants and a T-shirt while I write (and most of the rest of the time!) works for me. I'm pretty good about flossing my teeth though.

Out in the larger world, I no longer say yes if I really want to say no. I don't cater to manipulators, and I save my generosity for generous people, my goodness for good people. I don't try to impress others or compete with them. It's mind-blowing how much time I've managed to take back by letting go of these behaviors, and even though I backslide once in a while, I'm really proud of my growth.

I don't see a conflict between choosing to live the life that's best for me and supporting my family and friends and giving back to the world. If anything, I think I'm far better company when I'm being my authentic self.

If you're not there yet in your own life, and you're not even sure if you want to be, it's okay. Reinvention is a choice, not a requirement. And it's not a race. Finish reading this book and tuck it away for a while, physically or virtually. One day it might call out to you, and you'll read it again. When you get to the place where not going after your dream is more painful than actually going for it, you'll know it's time, just like I knew all those years ago when I was watching my daughter's swim practice.

When that tidal wave hits you, you'll be ready.

MEASURING SUCCESS

Not every dream will pay your bills. If I were in charge of the world, it would, but sadly I have no clout at all in this arena.

Not every dream will make you famous, though I have to admit personally I'm okay with that. My *Must Love Dogs* movie experience cured me of any craving I might have had for fame. I saw how hard it was for the actors to hang on to a slice of the everyday life the rest of us take for granted, how much work it was to surround themselves in a little bubble of normal, protected from everybody who wants a piece of them. How challenging it was to be good parents bringing up normal kids, to not live and breathe as celebrities. Granted there are tremendous perks to being famous, but it can also shrink your life and get in the way of your ability to connect with people.

Success might mean that you've managed to find a way to fit your dream into your life. You're painting three nights a week after the kids are in bed. You're hanging on to your day job, but working weekends for a catering company and soaking up every skill you can learn until the day you can start one of your own.

I'm grateful that I've been able to support myself with my writing for over a decade now, and that my loyal readers continue to welcome my next book. And I'm proud that I wake up every day and do the work I most want to do, and that I continue to try with all my heart and soul and brain power and elbow grease to raise the bar and become a better writer with each book. These are my measures of success.

A few books ago, a surprised new editor said to me, "Wow, it's still all about the writing for you, isn't it?" Absolutely. And the day it isn't, the day I've lost that passion, I hope I have the good sense to go find something else I can love just as much as I've loved writing books.

Sheryl Trainor might well be the world's only professional artist-slash-gas station owner. She fell in love with Vermont and its art scene, but needed to find a way to afford to live there. As she says, "I was able to buy my business only because a small door opened in the universe long enough for me to jump through."

In the late '90s, Mobil Oil Corp. decided to be proactive in promoting diversity, and so they offered a way for women and minorities to move from being managers of its corporate stores to independent gas station owners. Coincidentally, Sheryl had recently picked up a part-time job at a gas station to help pay her bills, and had quickly been promoted to manager. She knew nothing about business—she'd studied art and English literature in college. So she signed up for a small business class at a community college, wrote a business plan, and submitted it to Mobil.

It worked. Sheryl was the first person to make the leap and the only manager to be put into a station with no money down. Mobil lent her all the money and the operating capital necessary to buy her own gas station, something she never would have been able to do on her own. She bought her station in her dream location of Vermont, and she was later able to buy her own home there, too.

Nineteen years later, Sheryl is a talented printmaker whose work has been collected by museums and shown at prestigious galleries, and she serves on the board of a local arts organization. She still owns her gas station, too. At one point she opened a gallery in a small building at the edge of her gas station parking lot, with the dream of growing it until she could afford to retire from the station and pursue her life in the art world fulltime. She had some great shows, but it was never a real moneymaker, so when the economy tanked, she closed the gallery. Still, her gas station continues to support her life as an artist.

Mobil's program no longer exists, but if you're looking for similar opportunities, the U.S. Small Business Administration Office of Women's Business and Ownership is a great place to start, and you can Google up lots of other resources, too.

Diane Dillon might well be the world's only professional photographer-slash-flight attendant. She's got a great eye and shoots terrific portraits on a private beach near her home, and I've been lucky enough to have her take some of my author photos. But she's a single mom of two young sons, so she needs her other career as a flight attendant for the steady income and benefits. Her flying career allows her a flexible schedule and the chance to take photography classes all over the country. She books her photo sessions around the job that pays the bills.

Diane's mother, Charlotte Phinney, who I mentioned earlier in my *Today* story, began her career as a hair stylist when she was nineteen. After two years, she left to teach hairdressing, then returned and bought her original salon when she was twenty-four. "I had no business plan, only a desire to make my salon a place where women felt special and comfortable and would want to visit often. I poured everything I'd learned into it, using the skills I'd acquired teaching to educate my staff and encourage their growth. It taught me that if you give one hundred and fifty percent, you will get back more."

Charlotte suddenly found herself a single mom. "My husband's debt was a shock to me, and he was gone. I knew that I wanted to walk down the street in my hometown with my head held high, so I made arrangements to pay everyone over time." In order to do this, she realized she had to step up her income, so education in makeup was her next step. "It was an investment I couldn't afford, and yet couldn't afford not to make."

One Sunday, Charlotte was reading the newspaper and saw a jewelry auction at a high-end gift shop. She returned home with a car loaded with earrings. When she put them in her salon, they went flying out the door. She went from two earring racks to a mini boutique in her salon.

Next, Charlotte got a phone call from two talented stylists she'd trained right out of hairdressing school, who later moved to New York City and were wildly successful, with celebrity clients and nonstop schedules. But whenever they took a vacation, the networks and clients complained. So the stylists invited Charlotte to fill in for them for vacations and stay in their NYC apartment. Charlotte worked on television shows and Broadway plays and traveled with well-known celebrities, all the while shopping for her own boutique, which now had a separate location on the other side of town.

And then, even though both salon and boutique were doing really well, Charlotte realized that running them meant she no longer had time to do the things she loved the most: hair and makeup. So she closed the boutique and sold the salon, and she now sees a limited number of clients at the salon she once owned. She has reinvented herself once again by building a successful business doing airbrush makeup for television, and has worked her airbrush magic on everybody from President Obama to Diane Sawyer to Carole King. She also does hair and makeup for weddings, which she loves. "Success comes from seizing every opportunity that comes your way," Charlotte says.

ROLLER COASTER

I love happy endings, so nothing would give me more pleasure than to tell you that once you finally arrive at your reinvention destination, all your dreams will come true and you'll be living on easy street, set for life. Because that's where I am now, on the other side of that magical finish line. *Boyohboy* is my life perfect, and I can't wait for you to join me here in reinvention paradise. We'll have drinks! We'll chat about our stellar lives!

But I owe you the truth, and the truth is it doesn't work that way. There will always be challenges and, likely as not, they'll get even bigger. As the ancient Greek philosopher Heraclitus said, "The only thing constant is change." Just when you're getting comfortable, the destination you've happily arrived at can suddenly start shifting under your feet.

That's what happened to me. I was cruising along, represented by a powerful literary agent from a mighty agency that I both liked and respected, published by a series of big New York publishers that believed in my books and helped me make them better, and receiving advances for my novels that were substantial enough to live well on.

And then the publishing world began to get rocky, just like the music world and the newspaper world and so many others had before it.

I was one of the lucky authors. I had multi-book contracts and I was still being sent on book tour by my publisher and published in both hardcover and paperback, so I was able to put on my blinders and ignore the changes at first. Eventually, I couldn't help noticing my career stalling out, but I'm a glass half full kind of person, so I just shrugged it off and figured if I dug down deep and worked even harder than I was already working, I could make up for the shrinking energy and resources being put behind my books.

And then, after years of stability and support, it was jolting when a single one of my novels made the rounds through three separate editors, because the first two left the publishing house. I lost count of the in-house publicists disappearing through the revolving door— even their names began to blur. But the good news was that this was my final book under contract with this publisher, so I'd just find a better home for my books and me when I was free.

When the time came, my agent and I made the rounds, meeting with editors at the big publishing houses. I signed a two-book contract with the one who promised they'd put all their resources behind me to grow my readership and to get my career moving again in the right direction.

It didn't happen. I think they tried hard with the first book, but the things that used to work for traditional publishers trying to break out a book weren't working so well anymore. I wrote the second book I owed them. And then I found out that their entire plan for this book was to do all the things that hadn't worked for the first one. Even I couldn't find the glass half full in that. So I spoke up, verbally, and then in writing, and then in writing with lots of detail, even some bullet points.

Let's just say it didn't go over so well. A message was delivered to me via my literary agent that I should focus on writing the best book I could write and leave everything else to the professionals.

Oh, how I would have loved to.

Then my editor went off on a three-month maternity leave that would end just before my book came out, leaving her assistant, a very nice young woman a couple years out of college, responsible for the care of my novel, my baby. Less than a month before my publication date, I received an email from this very nice assistant telling me she was leaving publishing to start a takeout food business with a friend.

What a coincidence, I almost wrote back. *I'm leaving publishing to start a takeout food business, too!*

And now no one was in charge of my book.

It was such a low point. I was heartbroken, both for me and for the poor book I'd poured my heart and soul into. I'd spent thirteen years trying to be the hardest working author in the universe, and I felt excruciatingly let down by the institution that was literally feeding me. And paying my bills.

It gets worse. Around this time, I started receiving emails and calls from booksellers telling me they were having trouble ordering my backlist books that had been published by my last publisher. And then that last publisher went under and was bought out by another publisher who inherited all their titles. So in another huge bump in the road, these five backlist books went from being ignored to being part of a fire sale and were now owned by a new publisher that quickly demonstrated they had absolutely no interest in them.

One day right around this time it hit me: I simply can't do this again. I cannot let another publisher break my heart.

It gets better. Independent aka self-publishing had taken off and grown into a viable alternative. Authors in situations similar to mine were becoming hybrid authors—both traditionally and self-published. And in this new world, there was little of the cloak and dagger stuff I'd experienced in traditional publishing, where everything from money to marketing was kept secret. Indie authors were generously sharing everything they learned to help others on the same path. Via message boards and blogs and conferences, a great support system was bubbling up.

I'd already dipped a toe in this new pond, back when I first began to feel the changes. Ebooks were taking off like crazy and my readers were embracing them. Since I owned the rights to *Must Love Dogs*, I refor-matted it and uploaded the ebook on Amazon. I gave it away on Mother's Day to thank my readers for their support. No advertising, just an email blast, a post on Facebook and another one on Twitter. It had thirty-two thousand downloads in that one day and reached the number one spot on the Amazon free list, right next to *Fifty Shades of Gray* on the paid list. And now a whole bunch of people wanted to hear more from these characters. Amazing.

So the pieces of my new dream started to come together. I would find a way to get the rights to my backlist books reverted, and then I'd republish them with my own publishing company, which I'd call Marshbury Beach Books after the fictional town in my novels. Then I'd turn *Must Love Dogs* into a series— my readers wanted more, series were becoming more popular, and it would be fun to have a new kind of writing challenge since I'd never written a series. After that, I'd just keep writing, maybe even that nonfiction book about reinvention I'd wanted to write for years.

I hired a lawyer to help me begin the arduous process of getting the rights to my backlist reverted. But this time I did it the smart way. I reached out to a wonderful organization I belong to, Novelists, Inc., which has a legal fund for its members I could apply to for help subsidizing my efforts. NINC had a list of lawyers, and once I'd chosen one, they even made the initial contact for me.

I finished writing a draft of Book 2 of the new *Must Love Dogs* series. My agent not only read it, but also gave me helpful editorial advice. We seemed to be on the same page in terms of the steps I needed to take to get my career back on track. I'd already self-published *Must Love Dogs* and *Multiple Choice* with her full knowledge and support. It seemed to me that if I could get my career moving again, it would only benefit us both down the road.

And then one day on the phone, my agent informed me that in order to continue to be represented by this mighty agency, I would have to turn over fifteen percent of the proceeds of my about-to-be self-published book to said agency. Not only that, but I would have to publish it exclusively through Amazon, because the agency had a system in place with them where I could check a box and their fifteen percent would go straight to them, no muss, no fuss.

There was no deal, no sale. There would be no self-publishing assistance, no special treatment from Amazon to give my books an extra push, no marketing. I would be paying fifteen percent of my profits—forever—simply for the privilege of being represented by a big name agency. And this might well turn out to be representation in name only, since it was made clear to me that the mighty agency's subagents could not be expected to devote time and energy to selling rights to works that were not traditionally published.

It was wrong, ethically and financially, and I just couldn't do it. I Googled and searched message boards and was introduced to the term revenue grabbing.

To say it rocked my world would be an understatement. I was stunned, in part because I had several author friends traveling the same road, friends whose agents were supporting their indie journeys to get their careers back on track in a big way, and only commissioning the sales of subrights like foreign and audio and film.

A lawyer at another organization I'm a member of looked over my breakup papers furnished by the agency, and told me to look on the bright side, they never would have bothered if they didn't smell money. I was hardly a big fish at this agency, so in my mind it was more about getting caught in the crossfire as agents and publishers alike try to reinvent themselves and stay relevant in these quickly changing times.

I cried. A lot. At one point, I remember Googling Elisabeth Kübler-Ross's five stages of grief and realizing that I was cycling through them all, from denial to anger to bargaining to depression to acceptance. And then, once I finished wallowing and being pathetic, I shook it off and got back to work, more determined than ever.

As much as this whole thing totally, totally sucked, as much as it felt like my entire support system had been pulled out from under me, I never once questioned that I would continue writing. That's the definition of passion. And I never once questioned that my readers would want to read my next book, no matter how it was published. That's the definition of awesome.

If you're having a bad day/month/year, I hope my story just made you feel better! I tell it not to point fingers or to badmouth anyone, but in the spirit of those indie authors who have so generously shared information to help others coming up behind them on the road.

ONWARD AND UPWARD

I loved having a savvy, formidable literary agent advocating for me, and a connected group of terrific subagents going after foreign and film rights. I loved working with publishing teams made up of smart people who knew how to help me make my books better and had the clout to get my books much wider distribution than I could ever get on my own.

All ten of my traditionally published novels were chosen as Indie Next picks, a monthly list voted on by independent booksellers all over the country of the upcoming books they're most excited about. That bookseller support has been a huge gift to my career. I've done my best to return that support, and some of these booksellers have become my friends. So one of the most painful parts of walking away from traditional publishing was that my books would not be as available to these booksellers as they were before, and not at the deep discounts publishers could offer. There's nothing I can do about that. Looking back, I think it's one of the reasons I took so long to jump.

If the right literary agent comes along, one who gets where I'm going and can support my new journey in a meaningful way, that would be great. But I'm in no rush, and it's been both good to take a break to think about what I'll need moving forward, as well as empowering to take control of my own career.

I consider myself a hybrid author, both traditionally and self-published. If the right traditional publishing offer comes along, especially one that would get my paper books into bookstores in a more widespread way than I can on my own, I'd absolutely work with a traditional publisher again. As Guy Kawasaki, the former chief evangelist of Apple, said about his own hybrid author career, "I'm not for sale, but I am absolutely for rent."

But the magic for me is that I don't need it anymore.

Jumping off the traditional publishing treadmill I'd been on since 2000 meant making some short-term sacrifices, the biggest of which was letting go of the money it provided. But my self-published checks come monthly, not twice a year, and I get much higher percentages of sales without sharing a percentage. The income gap is closing.

I now own seven of my twelve books, including this one. I control pricing and promotion, and I can balance my need to earn a living with making my books available to my loyal readers at the best price I can offer them. I can add fresh content and switch excerpts and change covers any time I want. By the time I have ten indie-published books, I think Marshbury Beach Books and I will be doing just fine.

But already I'm happy. Instead of waiting for the next thing to go wrong, instead of feeling like I can't get close enough to my own career to move it in the right direction, I wake up every day and get right to work. I'm ridiculously busy, but I'm learning so many new things about writing and publishing and connecting, and I spend all day (and often a chunk of the night) doing the work I was born to do.

SERIAL REINVENTION

It's easy to fall into the trap, as I did, of thinking that once you've reinvented your life, you're all set. That old Kenny Rogers song was giving us good advice when it told us we have to know when to hold 'em and know when to fold 'em.

Robin Kall was the host of Reading with Robin, a radio show devoted to readers and the books they love. As Robin interviewed authors, readers could call in and chat with them, too, as well as win copies of their newest book. It was a great format that allowed Robin's personality to shine through, and the show had plenty of loyal fans.

Right around its ten-year anniversary, Robin hosted her final radio show. "It was time," she said. As much as she'd found the work she loved, the format was no longer making sense in the changing world around her. So Robin is now "reinventing the whole book platform so it's a fit." She's talking to another radio station about recording podcasts there, which will give her broadcast quality interviews and another place to host them in addition to her own site. She has also ramped up the book events she hosts, and is beginning to expand them geographically.

Robin is working on a brand new venture, too, but even though I tried to get it out of her, she's keeping it secret for now, allowing the idea to incubate as she does her initial research.

Satellite Sisters, created by the five real Dolan sisters—Julie, Liz, Sheila, Monica and Lian—began life as a one hour weekly radio show and website in 2001. The goal of the show was to bring real conversation from real women to a national audience.

In 2003, the show moved to ABC Radio and went from a one-hour, taped weekly show to a three-hour live daily show, six days a week. At its peak on air, Satellite Sisters ran on over 100 stations and had a million listeners a week.

When parent company Disney sold off ABC radio in 2008, the Satellite Sisters found themselves without a home on the radio, so they went to work on the web. As one of the early adapters of podcast technology, they were in a good place to switch to an all-digital distribution system, but it wasn't easy for them to learn a whole new business like digital content.

"Radio was a traditional, understandable business model. The digital world was like the Wild West," said Lian Dolan, who acts as executive producer and managing editor of Satellite Sisters. "It did feel like we had to start at the very bottom again and that was exhausting, but we knew our audiences wanted to stay connected. We weren't technical whizzes, but we decided that if we went to enough free classes at the Apple

Store, we could probably figure out how to produce, edit and distribute a podcast ourselves. At one point, my sister Liz, the marketing genius, actually bought a book called *Facebook for Dummies*. It was humbling, and we all had to go back to our pre-radio jobs for regular income, but we launched the podcast and hoped our people would find us. They did."

"Hang in," Lian said when I asked her for reinvention advice to pass along. "Change can take longer than you think. Make sure you love what you're doing so you have the emotional energy to stay focused."

In 2005, Ann Roth was a Kit Cat Girl in a production of *Cabaret*. The heel on one of her dance shoes came off, so she borrowed some automotive glue from her dance partner. As she was gluing the shoe back together that night, she decided to take apart a few old pairs of shoes in her closet and redesign them.

She was hooked. She took a sewing class and bought a book on making shoes and learned how to make a pair from scratch. She was in love with espadrilles, and they were popular that year, so she bought some cheap ones and ripped off the tops and re-made them with blue and white toile. She added silver sequins, coordinating navy satin trim, navy cotton insoles, and matching toile ribbons.

Then an avalanche of ideas started pouring into her head. "I'd have shoe ideas in the shower or as I was falling asleep, and I'd write everything down in a journal. I probably had one hundred ideas those first few weeks alone. It was like I had unlocked some secret hidden shoe world in my brain, and I was totally in awe and excited about everything."

Ann wore her creations to work. Friends and family saw them and wanted their own custom shoes. When strangers began to stop her on the street, Ann launched her business. "I never went to design school. I've had to teach myself how to draw (and it still looks like a third grader draws my sketches), and even though I had a business degree, I knew absolutely nothing about manufacturing and the world of shoes. Thank God for Google and nice people willing to help me learn!"

At its peak to date, Ann Roth Shoes were carried in over fifty stores across the US as well as one in Europe. "Then 2008 happened and businesses began to close their doors." Ann lost several accounts each season and orders decreased significantly. And then the factory she had been working with in Spain closed their doors, taking with them over $40,000 worth of shoes she had ordered and paid for. It was a huge blow for a small business, and Ann had to go back to a desk job for a while to recover financially.

When Ann gave birth to her daughter, Molly— "Who knew children are even better than shoes!"—she began to use Molly's naptime to rebuild her business. Ann found a new factory and has launched a new lower-priced line of truly fabulous wedges and espadrilles. She also offers private consultations to aspiring shoe designers trying to break into the business.

"The biggest piece of advice I have for any aspiring business owner," Ann says, "is don't make decisions in a hurry or out of fear. Every mistake I made was a decision made in a hurry because I was afraid of missing out on something.

"But right alongside that advice, I would also say if you have a dream, take action. Take small steps, very small if necessary, but do take that first step as soon as you can."

Ann's favorite quote is also one of my favorites: "Whatever you do, or dream you can, begin it. Boldness has genius and power and magic in it."—Johann Wolfgang von Goethe

HASTA LA VISTA, ISLA

I'm standing in a circle of shade on cobblestones shaped like dog bones. Peter, Paul and Mary are serenading me with a seriously retro imaginary version of "Leaving on a Jet Plane."

I'm waiting for my taxi so I can catch the first ferry of the day to Cancún and then fly home to Atlanta. I'm relieved the tuxedo cat hasn't shown up to make me feel worse than I already feel about not taking her home with me. I'm even more relieved to have learned that a woman named Lupita Moreno is as devoted to the cats on Isla Mujeres as Alison Sawyer Current is to the dogs.

I can't wait to see my family, but the beach is my happy place, and a part of me wants to stay and tell them to jump on a plane and meet me here. I woke up extra early this morning and made my way to the walk-through balcony outside my door. I stood facing a charcoal Caribbean until streaks of salmon cut through the pale gray sky, and then I drank in the sunrise along with the last of my Trader Joe's coffee.

The taxi arrives. I make the ferry in plenty of time and spend the twenty-minute ride gazing at the ocean through a salt-spattered window. But when I roll my suitcase down the ramp and out to the pickup area at the ferry terminal in Cancún, there's no one holding a sign with my name on it waiting to greet me.

It's Mexico, I'd say with a shrug if I didn't have a plane to catch. It's just after 7 A.M. The other ferry passengers jump into their waiting vehicles and head for wherever they're going. With every minute that passes in this dark parking garage-like area, I feel more alone and creeped out. I shake my head and wave off offers of rides from men who are either taxi drivers or the "pirates" I've been warned about that will try to confuse me into thinking they're my ride and then overcharge me for airport transportation that's already been paid for.

I have a phone number for the shuttle service. But I've been communicating only via the Internet since I got here, and if I turn on my phone while I'm still in Mexico, crazy amounts of data will download and cost me hundreds of dollars. I spy an old payphone off in a corner, but even if it works, which is a big if by the looks of it, the thought of trying to navigate it in Spanish and figure out the pesos is more than I can deal with so early in the morning.

One final straggling family is rolling their suitcases down the ramp to the pickup area. I'm just about to ask if I can hitch a ride with them to the airport, when a white van comes screeching into the parking lot.

The driver jumps out. My spirits lift as he slams the door and jogs toward me, tucking his shirt in while holding a white sign with his chin. He stops and holds up the sign in my direction. On it is the name of another woman from the conference. I remember that last night, while we all compared our flight times at the final party, she said she'd changed her pickup time so she could sleep in for an extra hour.

"That's me!" I yell, and I give the driver a big smile.

He looks at me skeptically, or maybe I only imagine it. He pulls out a clipboard and shows me his list of pickup names and times. And there I not only see my name, but that I'm scheduled to be driven to the Cancún airport right around the time my flight will be landing in Atlanta.

I can't remember how to say wrong, or whether time would be *la hora* or *el tiempo*, so I point to my name and then the time and then tell him in my pitiful Spanish that there is *un problema* and I need to go now.

"Thank you," he says in perfect English. "You have just made my day shorter."

He throws my suitcase into the back of the van and slides open the passenger door for me. It's Mexico, so as soon as we start heading for the airport, I tell him my fare has been paid, just in case he's thinking about trying to double charge.

He looks straight ahead. "Two thousand dollars American. Or I drop you off at the Mexican jail."

I'm pretty sure he's only kidding, but my heart skips a beat anyway as my body clicks into fight or flight mode.

I fake a yawn. "It's way too early in the morning for Mexican jail jokes."

"The tip is not included," he says.

"Fine." I reach into my bag and hand him an early tip in American dollars.

He laughs a big laugh and instantly we are friends. His name is Carlos and he once owned a successful restaurant in Cancún. He started drinking his profits and then ramped it up to drugs and gambling. He lost the restaurant, as well as everything else he owned. But he tells me he fought a hard fight and managed to stop doing the things that cost him his restaurant. He tells me he loves his family, and because of them, he couldn't give up.

"I must work very hard for a very long time to give them the life they deserve," he says. "But I will do it."

I believe him. And then he asks about my life, and when I tell him I used to be a teacher and now I'm an author, he asks me to write down my name for him. I rummage in my bag until I dig up a dog-eared bookmark with pictures of my books on it. He asks me to sign it for him, and I tell him I'm sorry I don't have a copy of one of my books to give him.

"Are they on Amazon?" he asks.

"Yes," I say.

"I have my own Amazon account," he says proudly. "I will buy your book."

I tell him to save his money for his family, that I'll send him a copy through the shuttle service when my next book is finished.

"Make sure you write Carlos on it," he says, "so nobody else takes it."

I get through security without a hitch and head for the restroom. The restroom attendant is about my age, and I give her my best, "*Hola. Buenos días.*" She makes a sound that might be a greeting. Her sad eyes pass right by mine and she looks away.

After I finish drying my hands, I dig through my bag for all the pesos I have left, which are only going to end up in my junk drawer if I take them home with me. I don't think it's very much money, and I'm certainly not going to attempt to count it to find out. When I hand it to her, she smiles a big, genuine smile.

Another woman is at the sink, putting on lipstick. She's about our age, too, and I think, in a parallel universe, the three of us could have gone to high school together. She puts her lipstick in her purse, pulls out her wallet, and hands her pesos over, too.

I don't know which one of us is happier, the restroom attendant or me. I think I've found my calling. I'm going to stay in this restroom all day long, pretending to give pesos to the attendant over and over again until she's absolutely rolling in dough, until she can buy a house and a car and quit this stupid job even if she loves it.

But of course I don't. The other woman and I say *adiós* and roll our carry-ons out into the terminal and start to chat. She's just finished spending a week in Cancún with a group of college friends that get together once a year. Her friends went home two days ago, but she stayed so she could have some time to herself. Her day job is elder care, but she's working toward reinventing herself in floral design, taking a small business class and working weekends and holidays for a local florist.

I tell her about the conference, and she pulls out a receipt and writes down the addresses of my website and the We Move Forward website on the back of it. I glance up at the departure screen and see that my flight is boarding. I say a quick goodbye and start to run. I'm almost to my gate before I realize we haven't even exchanged names.

On my flight home, I think about how cool it would be to just travel the world and talk to interesting people. At airports and on the road and at conferences and workshops and the beach and the grocery store. To hear their reinvention stories and to share mine. To encourage them all, and to soak up their encouragement like the hot sun sparkling off the turquoise water on Isla Mujeres.

But I really, really need to get home and write this book.

SEE YOU ON REINVENTION ROAD

I can't believe it's almost finished. Writing this book has been a labor of love in a different way than my novels have been, and when I find myself still searching for more to share, I realize it's because I don't want to say goodbye.

So I won't. Instead I'm going to invite you over to my website, ClaireCook.com, where a gift from me is waiting for you: a free *Never Too Late* workbook. All you have to do is sign up for my newsletter to download it on the spot. You can read it online or save it to your desktop or print it out. My hope is that the workbook will help you stay on track in your reinvention.

Being on my newsletter list means that if I remember something I should have mentioned, or learn anything helpful, I can pass it along to you. I'll also keep you updated on new releases, events and giveaways.

I hope you'll stay in touch via Facebook and Twitter and Pinterest, too. But only after we've finished our two pages a day!

For years now, I've kept a pile of special books on my bedside table. Whenever I need a little bit of inspiration, or even a lot of calming down, I pick one up and flip through it again. I sometimes think of it as biblio self-medication, and I have to say it works pretty well. I'd be honored if you'd add this book to your own special pile.

I wish you much joy and success in your reinvention. Keep me posted! And shine on!

xxxxxClaire

REINVENTORS AND RESOURCES

(in order of appearance)

Janeen Halliwell (WeMoveForward.com)
Janna Zinzi (GoddessesRising.blogspot.com)
Tiffany Lanier (SunHorseWeddings.com)
Katherine McLeod (GettingUpThere.ca)
My Facebook Research Team
(Facebook.com/ClaireCookauthorpage)
Rhonda Johnson (CrowningGloryHair.com)
Candace Hammond (Fix-It-Sisters.com)
Mary Carwile (MaryCarwile.com)
Miriam Laundry (LaundryBooks.com)
ElizaJ (ElizaJ.com)
Lisa Koch (HeyLisa.com)
Jane Friedman (JaneFriedman.com)
The Passive Voice (ThePassiveVoice.com)
Publishers Weekly (publishersweekly.com)
Shelf Awareness (shelf-awareness.com)
Writers' Café (kboards.com)
Writer Unboxed (WriterUnboxed.com)
Amy Angelilli (AdventureProject.com)
Julia Rosien (GoGirlfriend.com)

Journeywoman (Journeywoman.com)
Hole in the Donut (HoleintheDonut.com)
Wanderlust and Lipstick
(WanderlustandLipstick.com)
Traveling Wine Chick (TravelingWineChick.com)
Solo Traveler Blog (SoloTravelerBlog.com)
Robbie Kaye (RobbieKaye.com)
Judi Powers (JudiPowersJewelry.com)
Angelina de Galdamez (HotelBackpackers.com)
Kim Kraushar (Interlude.com)
Katie Milton (KatieMilton.com)
Shelley Roberts (StrategyClicks.com)
Julie Fraga (Serendipity-Design.info)
Alison Sawyer Current (IslaAnimals.org)
Pam Kramer
(examiner.com/book-in-national/pamela-kramer)
Dr. Katie Billmaier (LapofLove.com)
Deb Witte (DomicileDecor.com)
Susan Odegaard Turner (TurnerHealthcare.com)
Sheryl Trainor (SherylTrainor.com)
U.S. Small Business Administration
Office of Women's Business Ownership
(http://www.sba.gov/offices/headquarter/wbo)
Charlotte Phinney (CharlottePhinney.com)
Novelists, Inc. (Ninc.com)
Robin Kall (ReadingwithRobin.com)
Satellite Sisters (SatelliteSisters.com)
Ann Roth (AnnRothShoes.com)

ACKNOWLEDGMENTS

I couldn't have written this book without all the fabulous women who shared their reinvention stories with me. Many thanks to everyone who took time out of their busy lives to reach out to me via Facebook, Twitter, email, and in person. Whether I used your story directly or indirectly, your generosity and honesty helped this book come alive, and I'm beyond grateful to you for it.

A big thank-you to Janeen Halliwell for inviting me to give the keynote at We More Forward. It was the perfect place at the perfect time, and the conference not only helped shape the narrative structure of this book, but the women I met there, both as speakers and attendees, enriched these pages, as well as my life.

Ginormous thanks to Ken Harvey, who just rocks as a reader, for so many insightful comments. Another big thank-you to Bruce Myers, who gave me a huge piece of the puzzle.

Many thanks to Jack Kramer for putting his finger right on the parts of this book that still needed work.

A great big thank-you to Beth Hoffman for her true blue support and encouragement.

A huge thank-you to Ann Roth for sharing not only her story, but her enthusiasm and ideas for this book.

Thanks to Kaden and Garet for always being there when I need you. And, as always, the biggest thank-you of all goes to Jake.

ABOUT CLAIRE

I wrote my first novel in my minivan at 45. At 50, I walked the red carpet at the Hollywood premiere of the adaptation of my second novel, *Must Love Dogs*, starring Diane Lane and John Cusack. I'm now the *New York Times* bestselling author of 15 books. If you have a buried dream, take it from me, it is NEVER too late!

I've reinvented myself once again by turning *Must Love Dogs* into a series and writing two nonfiction books, *Never Too Late: Your Roadmap to Reinvention (without getting lost along the way)* and *Shine On: How To Grow Awesome Instead of Old*, in which I share everything I've learned on my own journey that might help you in yours. I've also become a reinvention speaker, so if you know anyone who's looking for a fun and inspiring speaker, I hope you'll send them to http://ClaireCook.com/speaking/. Thanks!

I was born in Virginia, and lived for many years in Scituate, Massachusetts, a beach town between Boston and Cape Cod. My husband and I have recently moved to the suburbs of Atlanta to be closer to our two adult kids, who actually want us around again!

I have the world's most fabulous readers and I'm forever grateful to all of you for giving me the gift of this career. Midlife Rocks!

xxxxxClaire

HANG OUT WITH ME!
ClaireCook.com
Facebook.com/ClaireCookauthorpage
Twitter.com/ClaireCookwrite
Pinterest.com/ClaireCookwrite

Be the first to find out when my next book comes out and stay in the loop for giveaways and insider excerpts: ClaireCook.com/newsletter.

Looking for another Claire Cook book?

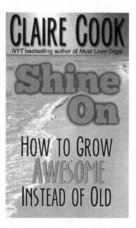

If you're a forty-to-forever woman, don't miss this motivating and inspiring book!

Join *New York Times* bestselling author Claire Cook on a transformative journey that will help you shake off all those worries about getting older and embrace what can be the most vibrant, creative and empowering chapter of your life.

Shine On: How to Grow Awesome Instead of Old speaks to women everywhere and is filled with Claire's trademark humor, heart, honesty and encouragement.

Life's a bit of a beach these days for Ginger Walsh, who finds herself single at 41 and back home living in the family FROG (finished room over the garage) in the fictional town of Marshbury. She's spent a few too many years in sales, and is hoping for a more fulfilling life as a sea glass artist, but instead is babysitting her sister's kids and sharing overnights with Noah, her sexy glassblower boyfriend with commitment issues and a dog Ginger's cat isn't too crazy about. And then a movie crew comes to town, along with a very cute gaffer.

You can almost smell the salt air as you take this rollicking ride with one slightly relationship-challenged single woman in *Life's a Beach*.

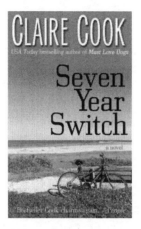

Just when Jill Murray has finally figured out how to make it on her own, her husband Seth is back, proving he can't even run away reliably. Now Jill has to face the fact that there's simply no way she can be a good mom without letting her ex back into her daughter Anastasia's life. They say that every seven years you become a completely new person. In ***Seven Year Switch*** it takes a Costa Rican getaway to help Jill make her choice—between the woman she is and the woman she wants to be.